GLOBAL RESPONSES TO HUMAN RIGHTS ISSUES A COMPREHENSIVE ANALYSIS

Global Responses to Human Rights Issues A Comprehensive Analysis

RAYAN MUSK

Mohammed Altaf Hussain

Contents

Table of Content

Introduction

Basic freedoms, thought about the bedrock of a fair and evenhanded society, have been at the very front of worldwide talk for a really long time. The advancement and insurance of these major privileges are basic for encouraging worldwide harmony, equity, and maintainable turn of events. In the perplexing woven artwork of our interconnected world, the infringement of common freedoms is an agitating reality that continues across borders, influencing people and networks in assorted ways. Understanding and tending to these infringement request a thorough examination of the worldwide reactions that have arisen to balance such offenses.

The mission for common freedoms has profound verifiable roots, with achievements like the Magna Carta and the General Statement of Basic liberties filling in as fundamental support points. Nonetheless, the contemporary worldwide scene is set apart by a bunch of difficulties, going from common and political freedoms to monetary, social, and social privileges. This far reaching examination plans to unwind the multifaceted snare of reactions made by countries, worldwide associations, and common society to face and moderate basic liberties infringement on a worldwide scale.

One critical part of this investigation includes inspecting the advancement of the global common freedoms system. The Unified Countries, laid out in the repercussions of The Second Great War, turned into a pot for producing an aggregate obligation to basic freedoms. The Widespread Statement of Basic liberties, embraced in 1948, set out a general norm for the innate respect and unavoidable freedoms of all individuals from the human family. Ensuing deals and shows, like the Global Contract on Common and Political Freedoms and the Worldwide Pledge on Financial, Social, and Social Privileges, further solidified the legitimate commitments of states in maintaining basic liberties.

In any case, the viability of these worldwide instruments depends on the ability of states to make an interpretation of their responsibilities into substantial activities. Subsequently, a basic assessment of the systems laid out to screen and uphold common freedoms becomes principal. The job of global bodies, for example, the Assembled Countries Basic liberties Committee, local associations like the European Court of Common freedoms, and specific organizations like the Worldwide Work Association are key to this investigation. Surveying their assets, shortcomings, and the difficulties they face in executing their commands gives a nuanced comprehension of the condition of worldwide reactions to basic freedoms issues.

Past the domain of formal foundations, the job of non-legislative associations (NGOs) and common society entertainers is basic in molding reactions to common liberties infringement. Support, mindfulness crusades, and grassroots developments frequently act as impetuses for change, coming down on legislatures and global bodies to address foundational treacheries. A made to order investigation of effective missions and the difficulties looked by common society entertainers reveals insight into the unique interchange between true channels and individuals driven drives.

The effect of globalization, set apart by expanded interconnectedness and reliance, has both positive and negative ramifications for basic liberties. On one hand, the dispersal of data and the enhancement of voices through computerized stages have engaged people to consider their states responsible. Then again, globalization has likewise worked with the cross-line development of capital, prompting financial variations that lopsidedly influence minimized networks. Dissecting the crossing point of globalization and common liberties discloses the complicated idea of the difficulties looked by the worldwide local area in creating responsive methodologies.

Besides, local variations in the advancement and security of basic liberties present an exceptional aspect to the extensive examination. Varieties in political frameworks, social standards, and authentic settings add to various methodologies and levels of obligation to basic freedoms across districts. The assessment of territorial associations and their adequacy in tending to neighborhood challenges gives bits of knowledge into the nuanced idea of reactions to basic freedoms issues.

In diving into the thorough examination, it is essential to investigate explicit topical regions where basic liberties infringement diligently happen. Issues, for example, orientation based brutality, victimization underestimated gatherings, ecological corruption, and the difficulties presented by arising advances require centered consideration. Understanding how these issues cross and the designated reactions contrived to address them adds to a more granular comprehension of the worldwide scene of common liberties.

1. Definition of Human Rights

The idea of basic liberties remains as a signal directing social orders toward the standards of equity, respect, and fairness. Established in hundreds of years of philosophical talk and solidified in global legitimate structures, common liberties address the unavoidable qualifications and opportunities intrinsic to each person by prudence of their humankind. Characterizing common liberties requires a nuanced investigation that includes the verifiable development of the idea, the general statements that revere them, and the essential rules that support their reality.

Verifiable Advancement of Common liberties

The starting points of common liberties can be followed back through the chronicles of history, with original minutes forming the direction of this central idea. The Magna Carta of 1215, frequently thought to be the most important phase in the foundation of individual privileges, laid the preparation by attesting that nobody ought to be denied of life, freedom, or property besides by the legitimate judgment of their companions or by the rule that everyone must follow. Notwithstanding, it was exclusively in the consequence of the barbarities of The Second Great War that the worldwide local area was prodded to formalize a far reaching structure for basic liberties.

The Widespread Statement of Basic liberties (UDHR), took on by the Unified Countries General Gathering in 1948, remains as a milestone record epitomizing the embodiment of common freedoms. Created following the abhorrences saw during the Holocaust and the pulverization of war, the UDHR expresses the innate nobility and equivalent freedoms of all individuals from the human family. Its introduction highlights the obligation to the advancement of widespread regard for and recognition of basic liberties and principal opportunities, without differentiation of any sort.

Essential Standards of Common liberties

At the center of the meaning of basic liberties lie a bunch of central rules that rise above social, political, and topographical limits. The guideline of all inclusiveness sets that basic freedoms are pertinent to each person, regardless of their identity, nationality, religion, or some other distinctive component. This all inclusiveness highlights the conviction that common freedoms are not honors gave by state run administrations but rather are, all things considered, intrinsic to individuals by ideals of their mankind.

The guideline of nature stresses that basic freedoms can't be given up, moved, or disavowed, even notwithstanding contrasting social practices or government strategies. People have these freedoms by the simple truth of being human, and no authority has the authentic ability to strip them away. Unavoidable nature fills in as a protect against erratic state activity and highlights the characteristic worth of every individual.

Relationship and unification comprise one more foundation standard, affirming that various classes of common freedoms are interconnected and commonly supporting. Common and political privileges, like the right to life and opportunity of articulation, are entwined with monetary, social, and social freedoms, including the right to schooling and a sufficient way of life. Perceiving their reliance highlights the all encompassing nature of basic freedoms, and tending to one classification is many times dependent upon the acknowledgment of others.

The rule of correspondence and non-separation highlights that all people are qualified for similar privileges and opportunities without segregation of any sort. This guideline rejects differentiations in view of race, orientation, religion, or some other status, guaranteeing that the advantages of basic freedoms gather to all citizenry evenhandedly. Taking out segregation encourages inclusivity and adds to the acknowledgment of an additional equitable and populist world.

The Authentic Job of Deals and Shows

While the UDHR laid the basic standards, resulting deals and shows play had a vital impact in making an interpretation of these standards into lawfully restricting commitments for states. The Global Contract on Common and Political Privileges (ICCPR) and the Worldwide Agreement on Monetary, Social, and Social Freedoms (ICESCR), both took on in 1966, extended and arranged the privileges verbalized in the UDHR. These deals, alongside others like the Show on the End of All Types of Oppression Ladies (CEDAW) and the Show on the Freedoms of the Youngster (CRC), comprise the foundation of the global basic liberties system.

Through the approval of these instruments, states focus on maintaining and regarding the freedoms revered inside them. The job of worldwide regulation in characterizing and defending common liberties is vital, as it gives a structure to responsibility and response for people whose freedoms might be disregarded. The presence of a far reaching legitimate design helps overcome any issues between the grand standards explained in statements and the viable requirement of common freedoms on the ground.

Challenges in Characterizing Basic liberties

While the standards and legitimate instruments are fundamental parts in the meaning of common freedoms, challenges continue making an interpretation of these goals into noteworthy real factors. Social relativism, for example, represents a test as some contend that basic liberties ought to be deciphered inside the setting of explicit social, strict, or cultural standards. Offsetting social responsiveness with the comprehensiveness of common freedoms stays a continuous discussion in the domain of characterizing and carrying out these privileges.

Additionally, the politicization of basic liberties frequently prompts particular requirement, where strong states might get away from responsibility for infringement while less powerful countries face investigation. The particular utilization of common freedoms norms sabotages the comprehensiveness and fairness of the idea, making a polarity among way of talking and practice. Tending to these difficulties requires a nuanced approach that recognizes social variety while maintaining the center rules that structure the pith of basic freedoms.

Contemporary Importance of Basic liberties

In the 21st 100 years, the significance of common liberties has just strengthened, with new difficulties arising in a time set apart by fast mechanical headways, worldwide interconnectedness, and developing types of administration. The advanced age presents the two open doors and dangers to common liberties, with issues like web-based security, opportunity of articulation in computerized spaces, and the moral ramifications of arising innovations reshaping the talk on freedoms.

Additionally, the diversity of common liberties has come to the very front, perceiving that people frequently face intensified types of segregation in view of numerous variables like orientation, race, and financial status. Endeavors to address common freedoms should hence take on a multifaceted focal point, recognizing the interconnectedness of different parts of character and the effect on a singular's admittance to privileges.

2. ## Historical Evolution of Human Rights

The verifiable development of common liberties is a convincing excursion through the records of time, a story woven by the aggregate goals for equity, nobility, and correspondence. Established in philosophical thoughts, formed by groundbreaking verifiable occasions, and solidified in worldwide legitimate systems, the idea of common liberties has gone through a significant development. This investigation takes us on a nuanced journey, following the achievements that established the groundwork for the acknowledgment and insurance of these key privileges.

Pre-Current Forerunners

The underlying foundations of common freedoms can be recognized in the antiquated and archaic periods, where scholars and rationalists wrestled with the possibility of innate privileges supplied to people. In antiquated Greece, the idea of "dikaiosyne" (equity) and the apathetic way of thinking highlighted the possibility that specific privileges were characteristic for human instinct. Essentially, the Roman legitimate idea of "jus gentium" (law of countries) perceived that specific standards applied generally, regardless of citizenship.

The Magna Carta of 1215 addresses a critical second in the development of individual freedoms. While basically a report stating the freedoms of the English noblemen against the inconsistent force of the ruler, it set out the rule that nobody ought to be denied of life, freedom, or property besides by the legal judgment of their friends or by the rule that everyone must follow. The Magna Carta, consequently, planted the seeds of impediments on monarchical power and gave an early look into the thought of individual privileges as a keep an eye on severe administration.

The Illumination and the Introduction of Present day Basic freedoms

The seventeenth and eighteenth hundreds of years saw a seismic scholarly shift with the Illumination, where rationalists upheld for reason, freedom, and individual privileges. Illumination masterminds like John Locke, Jean-Jacques Rousseau, and Voltaire added to the conceptualization of freedoms as intrinsic to people, originating before the rise of formalized legitimate instruments.

John Locke's "Two Compositions of Government" (1690) set that people had regular privileges, including life, freedom, and property, which preexisted and supplanted the foundation of political social orders. This way of thinking laid the preparation for later statements on the comprehensiveness of basic freedoms. The French Illumination, with its accentuation on "liberté, égalité, fraternité," further powered the talk on individual opportunities and correspondence.

American and French Transformations

The late eighteenth century gave testimony regarding progressive developments that completed the standards of the Illumination. The American Announcement of Autonomy in 1776 cherished the possibility that all men were made equivalent and supplied with unalienable freedoms, including life, freedom, and the quest for satisfaction. This essential report mirrored the impact of Edification thoughts in forming an early's comprehension country might interpret common freedoms.

Essentially, the French Insurgency of 1789 delivered the Statement of the Freedoms of Man and of the Resident, an original record broadcasting the innate privileges, everything being equal. This statement enunciated a bunch of individual privileges, including the right to freedom, property, security, and protection from persecution. Albeit at first bound to male residents, the statement laid a foundation for the more extensive battle for general freedoms.

Internationalization of Basic liberties in the twentieth Hundred years

The barbarities of The Second Great War, including the Holocaust and far reaching denials of basic freedoms, electrifies the global local area to lay out an extensive system for the security of common liberties. The consequence of the conflict saw the making of the Assembled Countries (UN) in 1945, laying the preparation for the internationalization of basic freedoms.

The Widespread Statement of Common freedoms (UDHR), embraced by the UN General Get together in 1948, remains as a turning point in the verifiable development of basic liberties. Drafted under the direction of figures like Eleanor Roosevelt, the UDHR broadcasted a typical norm of privileges for all individuals and put forward a dream of a reality where people appreciate independence from dread and need. The UDHR involves common, political, financial, social, and social freedoms, typifying the association and inseparability of basic liberties.

Post-WWII Legitimate Instruments

Expanding upon the UDHR, the post-The Second Great War period saw the codification of common liberties in legitimately restricting global instruments. The Worldwide Pledge on Common and Political Privileges (ICCPR) and the Global Agreement on Financial, Social, and Social Freedoms (ICESCR), both took on in 1966, further explained on unambiguous privileges and gave components to their requirement.

The territorial setting likewise assumed a critical part in the development of common freedoms. The European Show on Common freedoms (ECHR), laid out in 1950, made a territorial structure for the security of basic liberties in Europe. Also, the Between American Court of Common liberties and the African Contract on Human and People groups' Privileges arose to address basic freedoms worries inside their particular locales.

Basic freedoms in the Virus War Period

The Virus War period introduced a complicated setting for the advancement of basic freedoms. While the two superpowers, the US and the Soviet Association, advocated their political situation, allegations of denials of basic liberties were exchanged between them. The Helsinki Accords of 1975, endorsed by the US, the Soviet Association, and various different countries, denoted an endeavor to connect philosophical partitions and advance common freedoms.

Be that as it may, the Virus War additionally saw cases where basic freedoms were compromised for international interests. Notwithstanding these difficulties, the period added to the advancement of standards and instruments for tending to common liberties infringement on the worldwide stage.

The Development of Common freedoms Instruments

The foundation of global bodies committed to the assurance and advancement of common liberties further epitomizes the verifiable development of the basic freedoms system. The Assembled Countries Basic liberties Committee (UNHRC), made in 2006, succeeded the UN Commission on Common freedoms and planned to worldwide upgrade the advancement and assurance of basic liberties. Particular offices like the Worldwide Work Association (ILO) additionally assumed a vital part in tending to basic liberties worries with regards to work.

Common freedoms systems additionally stretch out to the territorial level, where bodies like the European Court of Basic liberties, the Between American Commission on Basic freedoms, and the African Court on Human and People groups' Privileges act as gatherings for arbitrating basic liberties cases. These instruments, alongside public common freedoms organizations, add to the requirement and acknowledgment of basic liberties across assorted settings.

Difficulties and Contemporary Points of view

Regardless of the huge steps in the authentic advancement of basic freedoms, challenges continue in the 21st hundred years. Issues like social relativism, particular implementation, and the effect of innovative progressions on security and opportunity require continuous talk and variation of basic liberties standards.

Social relativism suggests the conversation starter of whether common freedoms ought to be all around applied or on the other hand assuming they ought to be contextualized inside unambiguous social, strict, or cultural standards. Finding some kind of harmony between social responsiveness and maintaining the comprehensiveness of basic liberties stays a mind boggling challenge.

Particular requirement, frequently determined by international contemplations, raises worries about the fair-mindedness of the basic liberties system. The politicization of common liberties can bring about the sidelining of specific infringement while amplifying others, compromising the consistency and reasonableness of the framework.

The computerized age presents new difficulties, with issues like web-based security, opportunity of articulation in advanced spaces, and the moral ramifications of arising innovations reshaping the talk on freedoms. As innovation keeps on propelling, the basic freedoms system should adjust to address the advancing dangers and open doors introduced by the computerized scene.

3. Importance of Global Responses

In a period of extraordinary interconnectedness, the significance of worldwide reactions to common liberties issues couldn't possibly be more significant. The difficulties that defy mankind today — going from clashes and segregation to ecological emergencies and pandemics — rise above public boundaries. The perplexing trap of our globalized world requests coordinated endeavors, shared liability, and cooperative answers for address the complex issues that block the acknowledgment of all inclusive basic liberties. This investigation digs into the meaning of worldwide reactions in shielding common liberties, examining the job of global establishments, common society, and cooperative drives in molding an additional fair and evenhanded world.

Worldwide Common liberties Structure

At the core of worldwide reactions to common freedoms issues lies the global basic liberties system, an intricate embroidery of deals, shows, and statements. The Unified Countries, laid out in the result of The Second Great War, turned into the focal point for producing an aggregate obligation to basic freedoms. The Widespread Statement of Basic liberties (UDHR), took on in 1948, remains as a fundamental report that verbalizes the intrinsic respect and unavoidable freedoms of all individuals from the human family.

Resulting settlements, remembering the Worldwide Contract for Common and Political Privileges (ICCPR) and the Global Agreement on Monetary, Social, and Social Freedoms (ICESCR), further depict the lawful commitments of states in maintaining basic liberties.

The significance of this global structure lies in setting principles as well as in giving components to observing and implementation. The

Unified Countries Basic liberties Chamber (UNHRC), provincial common freedoms bodies, and concentrated organizations assume a critical part in examining state consistence and offering roads for review when infringement happen. The presence of a worldwide lawful design highlights the common obligation to the standards enunciated in these instruments and gives an establishment to responsibility.

Local and Multilateral Collaboration

The meaning of worldwide reactions is additionally highlighted by territorial and multilateral collaboration. Local associations, like the European Association (EU), the African Association (AU), and the Association of American States (OAS), assume crucial parts in tending to common liberties issues inside their particular circles. These associations give gatherings to discourse, participation, and joint activity, perceiving that challenges frequently require setting explicit reactions.

Multilateral participation is exemplified by cooperative endeavors to handle worldwide issues that influence common freedoms. Environmental change, for example, presents an ecological danger as well as intensifies existing imbalances and endangers the prosperity of weak networks. The Paris Understanding, embraced in 2015, mirrors a worldwide obligation to tending to environmental change all in all, perceiving its significant ramifications for basic freedoms, especially the right to a solid climate.

Common Society and Grassroots Developments

The significance of worldwide reactions stretches out past the domain of formal organizations to envelop the energetic job of common society and grassroots developments. Non-legislative associations (NGOs), support gatherings, and people on the ground frequently act as the impetuses for change, pointing out basic freedoms infringement and pushing for responsibility. The force of common society lies in its capacity to enhance voices, activate networks, and consider states and global bodies responsible.

Verifiable models, for example, the counter politically-sanctioned racial segregation development in South Africa or the worldwide mission against landmines, outline the extraordinary effect of common society in molding the basic freedoms plan. Developments like #MeToo and People of color Matter in the contemporary setting highlight the strength of grassroots activism in testing foundational treacheries and driving social change.

The significance of worldwide reactions is complicatedly attached to the acknowledgment that supportable advancement requires the dynamic cooperation and carefulness of common society entertainers.

Globalization and Interconnected Difficulties

Globalization, described by expanded monetary, social, and mechanical interconnectedness, has introduced the two valuable open doors and difficulties for basic liberties. The development of merchandise, capital, and data across borders has worked with financial development however has additionally complemented variations and weaknesses. The significance of worldwide reactions lies in exploring the perplexing elements of globalization to guarantee that it contributes emphatically to common liberties.

Monetary globalization, for example, has prompted the double-dealing of work in specific businesses and locales, presenting difficulties to one side to fair and simply working circumstances. The worldwide reaction to such difficulties requires administrative structures as well as cooperative endeavors to address the main drivers, remembering inconsistent power elements for the worldwide economy.

Likewise, the computerized age has delivered novel difficulties to security, opportunity of articulation, and admittance to data. The significance of worldwide reactions in this setting is clear in drives pointed toward laying out moral norms for arising advancements, directing web-based spaces, and protecting people from computerized freedoms mishandles. The interconnected idea of these provokes requires worldwide collaboration to plan compelling reactions that offset advancement with the assurance of crucial freedoms.

Basic liberties and Equipped Struggles

One of the most powerful outlines of the significance of worldwide reactions is seen with regards to furnished clashes. Wars and clashes, whether inner or worldwide, perpetually bring about common freedoms infringement for a gigantic scope. The worldwide reaction to such emergencies requires a diverse methodology, including discretionary endeavors, helpful intercessions, and responsibility systems.

Global philanthropic regulation, exemplified in the Geneva Shows and their Extra Conventions, gives a structure to safeguarding regular folks and non-warriors during furnished clashes. The foundation of worldwide criminal councils, like the Global Lawbreaker Court (ICC), highlights the obligation to guaranteeing responsibility for atrocities, destruction, and violations against humankind. The significance of worldwide reactions in struggle circumstances lies in alleviating prompt mischief as well as in cultivating manageable harmony, compromise, and the remaking of social orders broke by savagery.

Pandemics and General Wellbeing Emergencies

The worldwide reaction to pandemics and general wellbeing emergencies enlightens the interconnected idea of common liberties. The flare-up of illnesses, like the Coronavirus pandemic, represents how wellbeing crises can resonate universally, affecting economies, social designs, and individual prosperity. The significance of worldwide reactions in such situations is twofold: first, in the coordination of endeavors to contain the spread of the sickness and give clinical help, and second, in addressing the financial results to forestall fuel of existing imbalances.

Worldwide associations, including the World Wellbeing Association (WHO), assume a focal part in organizing worldwide reactions to pandemics. The fair appropriation of immunizations, admittance to medical care, and the insurance of weak populaces become fundamental contemplations that rise above public lines. The interconnectedness of wellbeing, monetary, and social aspects highlights the significance of an aggregate and facilitated worldwide reaction to shield the right to wellbeing and prosperity.

Chapter 1

The State of Human Rights Worldwide

The condition of basic freedoms overall stands at the intersection of progress and determined difficulties, mirroring the powerful transaction of international movements, financial incongruities, and advancing worldwide emergencies. This exhaustive examination explores through the diverse scene of common freedoms, looking at the two headways and mishaps across locales, topical regions, and the unpredictable snare of global relations. From common and political privileges to monetary, social, and social aspects, the assessment of the condition of basic liberties highlights the basic of aggregate activity to resolve fundamental issues and shield the innate pride of people around the world.

Worldwide Patterns and Difficulties

As the world stands up to the intricacies of the 21st 100 years, a few overall worldwide patterns and difficulties shape the condition of basic freedoms. One conspicuous pattern is the ascent of dictatorship and the disintegration of majority rule organizations in different areas of the planet.

States, both laid out majority rules systems and arising powers, wrestle with issues of responsibility, straightforwardness, and the assurance of urban space, presenting difficulties to the acknowledgment of common and political freedoms.

Besides, the effect of environmental change and ecological debasement presents another outskirts in common liberties talk. Dislodging because of environment related occasions, dangers to livelihoods, and natural treacheries excessively influence weak networks, adding criticalness to the requirement for a rights-based way to deal with ecological security.

The Coronavirus pandemic, a worldwide wellbeing emergency of exceptional scale, has revealed the delicacy of wellbeing frameworks, fueling prior disparities and highlighting the diversity of basic freedoms. The right to wellbeing, admittance to data, and financial prosperity have become central focuses in the worldwide reaction to the pandemic, uncovering both cooperative endeavors and weaknesses in tending to general wellbeing emergencies.

Common and Political Privileges

The condition of common and political privileges overall mirrors a mind boggling interaction of progress and difficulties. While steps have been made in progressing popularity based administration, occurrences of breaking faith, disintegration of law and order, and crackdowns on contradict persevere in different locales. The concealment of free discourse, limitations on tranquil gathering, and goes after on autonomous media hinder the activity of principal privileges in both laid out vote based systems and totalitarian systems.

A striking concern is the ascent of computerized tyranny, where states exploit mechanical progressions to watch and control their populaces. The abuse of reconnaissance advances, online control, and dangers to security feature the developing difficulties to common freedoms in the computerized age.

The security of minimized gatherings, including ethnic and strict minorities, LGBTQ+ people, and native networks, stays a basic part of common and political privileges. Separation, viciousness, and fundamental hindrances keep on hindering the full satisfaction in privileges by these gatherings, requiring coordinated endeavors to address underlying imbalances and advance inclusivity.

Monetary, Social, and Social Freedoms

The condition of monetary, social, and social freedoms is set apart by relentless variations in admittance to essential necessities and open doors. Disparity in abundance dispersion, deficient social wellbeing nets, and hindrances to schooling and medical care add to the propagation of destitution and prevent the acknowledgment of crucial freedoms.

The Coronavirus pandemic has exacerbated existing financial disparities, excessively influencing weak populaces. Disturbances to schooling, loss of occupations, and lacking medical care foundation highlight the interconnectedness of financial, social, and social freedoms with more extensive general wellbeing and prosperity contemplations.

Work privileges stay a point of convergence, with issues, for example, problematic business, youngster work, and manipulative working circumstances presenting difficulties to the security of laborers. The significance of fair wages, safe workplaces, and social assurances is highlighted by the worldwide development supporting for the pride and privileges of laborers across different businesses.

Orientation based Separation and Brutality

The condition of common freedoms overall is profoundly laced with the inescapable issue of orientation based segregation and viciousness. Ladies and orientation minorities keep on confronting foundational disparities, segregation, and viciousness across different circles of life. The tenacious orientation pay hole, obstructions to training and work, and the pervasiveness of orientation based savagery highlight the requirement for designated endeavors to address orientation differences.

Legitimate structures and worldwide shows, like the Show on the Disposal of All Types of Oppression Ladies (CEDAW), give an establishment to advancing orientation equity. In any case, the authorization and execution of these structures stay lopsided, featuring the requirement for far reaching methodologies to address well established orientation standards and generalizations.

Progressions in LGBTQ+ freedoms in certain districts stand out from the mistreatment and segregation looked by LGBTQ+ people in others. The decriminalization of same-sex connections, legitimate acknowledgment of orientation personality, and the security of LGBTQ+ privileges arise as sure patterns, however challenges continue, requiring a worldwide obligation to cultivating inclusivity and combatting segregation in view of sexual direction and orientation character.

Basic liberties in Struggle Zones

Outfitted clashes and political agitation keep on being cauldrons of basic freedoms infringement, moving the global local area's capacity to forestall and address abominations. The utilization of synthetic weapons, assaults on regular folks, constrained dislodging, and the enlistment of youngster troopers address horrifying infringement of worldwide philanthropic regulation, requesting responsibility and equity for casualties.

The condition of common freedoms in struggle zones highlights the significance of worldwide participation to address the main drivers of contentions and to work with conciliatory goals. The assurance of regular citizens, philanthropic access, and the arraignment of war wrongdoings through systems like the Worldwide Crook Court (ICC) are fundamental parts of worldwide reactions to denials of basic liberties in struggle circumstances.

Outcast and Traveler Freedoms

The predicament of exiles and transients features the condition of common freedoms at the crossing point of political, social, and monetary difficulties. Constrained uprooting, whether because of contention, oppression, or natural variables, represents a basic helpful concern. The option to look for haven, security from refoulement, and admittance to stately day to day environments are fundamental parts of evacuee privileges that request worldwide consideration and collaboration.

Transients, especially those in sporadic or tricky circumstances, frequently face infringement of their privileges, including double-dealing, segregation, and lacking admittance to fundamental administrations. Extensive and privileges based relocation strategies, combined with global participation, are critical to tending to the weaknesses looked by travelers and guaranteeing that their common freedoms are maintained all through their excursions.

The Job of Worldwide Organizations and Instruments

Global organizations and components assume an essential part in molding the condition of basic liberties around the world. The Assembled Countries, through its different bodies like the UN Common freedoms Chamber, fills in as a stage for discourse, checking, and the advancement of basic liberties principles. Particular offices, including the Global Work Association (ILO) and the World Wellbeing Association (WHO), add to propelling explicit components of basic liberties, for example, work freedoms and the right to wellbeing.

Local associations, like the European Association, the African Association, and the Association of American States, supplement worldwide endeavors by tending to common freedoms worries inside their particular circles. Territorial courts and councils, including the European Court of Common liberties and the Between American Court of Basic freedoms, give roads to people and networks to look for review for common freedoms infringement.

The Worldwide Crook Court (ICC) fills in as a basic system for responsibility in instances of slaughter, atrocities, and violations against mankind. Be that as it may, challenges connected with the requirement of ICC choices and the issue of exemption continue, highlighting the requirement for supported endeavors to reinforce worldwide equity systems.

The Job of Common Society and Grassroots Developments

Common society and grassroots developments comprise basic problem solvers in molding the condition of common liberties around the world. Non-legislative associations (NGOs), support gatherings, and people on the ground frequently act as the voice of the underestimated, testing severe systems, upholding for strategy changes, and preparing networks.

Verifiable models, like the counter politically-sanctioned racial segregation development in South Africa or the social equality development in the US, feature the groundbreaking force of common society in testing foundational treacheries. Contemporary developments, including #MeToo and Fridays for Future, highlight the flexibility and strength of grassroots activism in driving social change and considering people with significant influence responsible for common liberties infringement.

Difficulties and Open doors in the Computerized Age

The advanced age presents the two difficulties and open doors for the condition of common liberties around the world. While mechanical progressions empower the spread of data, network, and activism, they likewise present new elements of hazard, including computerized reconnaissance, online control, and the weaponization of innovation to smother contradict.

The right to security faces phenomenal difficulties as observation advances become more modern and unavoidable. State-supported observation, corporate information assortment, and the control of advanced stages for political purposes bring up key issues about the assurance of people's confidential lives and the requirement for strong lawful structures to protect computerized privileges.

Opportunity of demeanor, a foundation of common and political privileges, faces new difficulties in the computerized domain. Online control, disinformation crusades, and the concealment of disagreeing voices via virtual entertainment stages feature the requirement for procedures to adjust the receptiveness of computerized spaces with the security of majority rule values and common liberties.

1.1 Overview of Current Human Rights Issues

The contemporary world wrestles with a bunch of basic freedoms challenges, mirroring the powerful interchange of political, social, financial, and innovative powers. This outline digs into the multi-layered scene of current common freedoms issues, investigating the intricacies and interconnectedness that characterize the condition of basic liberties universally. From common and political freedoms to financial, social, and ecological aspects, the assessment of these issues highlights the dire requirement for aggregate activity, global collaboration, and a restored obligation to maintaining the poise and privileges of each and every person.

Common and Political Freedoms

One of the unmistakable subjects in the ongoing basic freedoms scene is the diligent disintegration of common and political privileges in different areas. Tyranny, powered by the ascent of egalitarian pioneers and the control of vote based processes, represents a critical test to the security of individual freedoms. Occurrences of political constraint, shortening of opportunity of articulation, and crackdowns on disagree illustrate the contracting space for common society in both laid out majority rules systems and absolutist systems.

Computerized tyranny further worsens concerns connected with common and political privileges. States exploit progressed reconnaissance innovations to screen residents, smother political resistance, and diminish protection privileges. The weaponization of advanced stages for disinformation crusades, online oversight, and the utilization of man-made consciousness in state reconnaissance highlight the developing difficulties to common freedoms in the computerized age.

Besides, separation and viciousness against underestimated bunches endure, with ethnic and strict minorities, LGBTQ+ people, and native networks confronting increased dangers to their common and political freedoms. Maintaining the standards of non-segregation, balance, and equity becomes urgent in countering the fundamental hindrances that obstruct the full acknowledgment of these freedoms for defenseless and underestimated populaces.

Monetary, Social, and Social Privileges

Financial, social, and social privileges stay fundamental to the talk on common liberties, with persevering variations in admittance to essential necessities and open doors. Financial imbalance, lacking social security nets, and hindrances to training and medical services add to the propagation of neediness, upsetting the acknowledgment of principal privileges.

The effect of the Coronavirus pandemic has exacerbated existing financial disparities, lopsidedly influencing weak populaces. Disturbances to training, loss of jobs, and insufficient medical care framework highlight the interconnectedness of financial, social, and social freedoms with more extensive general wellbeing and prosperity contemplations. Endeavors to address these difficulties require far reaching techniques that focus on inclusivity, fair asset appropriation, and the insurance of monetary and social privileges.

Work freedoms likewise stay a point of convergence in the contemporary common liberties scene. Issues, for example, unsafe business, kid work, and shifty working circumstances endure, requesting worldwide consideration regarding guarantee fair wages, safe work spaces, and social securities for laborers. As the idea of work develops despite mechanical headways, adjusting lawful structures to safeguard the privileges of laborers becomes principal.

Orientation Based Segregation and Brutality

Orientation based segregation and brutality keep on being inescapable worldwide difficulties, requesting dire consideration and purposeful endeavors for fundamental change. Ladies and orientation minorities face fundamental imbalances, segregation, and viciousness across different circles of life. The orientation pay hole, obstructions to schooling and work, and the commonness of orientation based viciousness feature the requirement for designated mediations to address orientation incongruities.

Lawful structures and worldwide shows, like the Show on the End of All Types of Oppression Ladies (CEDAW), give fundamental devices to advancing orientation balance. In any case, the execution of these structures stays lopsided, underscoring the requirement for supported endeavors to challenge well established orientation standards and generalizations.

While headways in LGBTQ+ privileges have been seen in certain districts, segregation and oppression endure in others. The decriminalization of same-sex connections, lawful acknowledgment of orientation character, and the security of LGBTQ+ privileges are positive patterns. Nonetheless, challenges remain, requiring a worldwide obligation to cultivating inclusivity and battling segregation in light of sexual direction and orientation personality.

Basic freedoms in Struggle Zones

Furnished clashes and political distress keep on being pots of basic liberties infringement, presenting significant difficulties to global harmony and security. The utilization of substance weapons, assaults on regular folks, constrained uprooting, and the enlistment of kid warriors address shocking infringement of global compassionate regulation. The security of regular folks, helpful access, and responsibility systems for atrocities become fundamental parts of worldwide reactions to denials of basic liberties in struggle circumstances.

The situation of displaced people and transients is one more basic element of common freedoms in struggle zones. Constrained dislodging because of contention, mistreatment, or ecological elements requests a rights-based way to deal with shelter, insurance from refoulement, and admittance to honorable everyday environments for uprooted populaces. Extensive and helpful procedures are significant to tending to the weaknesses looked by exiles and travelers and guaranteeing that their basic freedoms are maintained all through their excursions.

The Job of Global Foundations and Systems

Worldwide foundations and components assume a crucial part in molding the ongoing basic liberties scene. The Assembled Countries, through bodies like the UN Common freedoms Chamber, fills in as a stage for exchange, checking, and the advancement of basic liberties norms.

Local associations, like the European Association, the African Association, and the Association of American States, supplement worldwide endeavors by tending to common liberties worries inside their separate circles.

The Worldwide Crook Court (ICC) fills in as a basic system for responsibility in instances of decimation, atrocities, and violations against humankind. Notwithstanding, challenges connected with the authorization of ICC choices and the issue of exemption continue to happen, highlighting the requirement for supported endeavors to reinforce worldwide equity components.

Common society and grassroots developments keep on being essential problem solvers, testing severe systems, supporting for strategy changes, and preparing networks. Verifiable models, like the counter politically-sanctioned racial segregation development in South Africa or the social liberties development in the US, highlight the groundbreaking force of common society in testing fundamental treacheries. Contemporary developments, including #MeToo and Fridays for Future, show the versatility and strength of grassroots activism in driving social change and considering people with significant influence responsible for common liberties infringement.

Difficulties and Amazing open doors in the Advanced Age

The computerized age presents the two difficulties and open doors for the condition of basic freedoms around the world. While innovative headways empower the spread of data, network, and activism, they additionally present new elements of chance, including computerized reconnaissance, online oversight, and the weaponization of innovation to smother disagree.

The right to protection faces exceptional difficulties as observation innovations become more modern and inescapable. State-supported observation, corporate information assortment, and the control of computerized stages for political purposes bring up key issues about the security of people's confidential lives and the requirement for vigorous lawful structures to protect advanced freedoms.

Opportunity of demeanor, a foundation of common and political freedoms, faces new difficulties in the computerized domain. Online oversight, disinformation crusades, and the concealment of contradicting voices via web-based entertainment stages feature the requirement for procedures to adjust the transparency of advanced spaces with the insurance of majority rule values and common liberties.

1.2 Different Regions

The worldwide scene of common freedoms is innately assorted, molded by authentic, social, and international factors that add to particular difficulties across various districts.

This investigation dives into the nuanced woven artwork of common liberties issues, analyzing the exceptional elements and shared worries that portray different areas of the planet. From the Americas and Europe to Asia, Africa, and the Center East, every district wrestles with its arrangement of difficulties, highlighting the basic of setting explicit methodologies and global collaboration to cultivate an existence where common freedoms are generally safeguarded.

The Americas:

In the Americas, common freedoms issues manifest against a scenery of majority rule customs, financial variations, and verifiable heritages. While nations like Canada and the US maintain hearty basic freedoms systems, challenges persevere, especially with regards to racial imbalances and separation. Fundamental issues like police savagery against minimized networks, as featured by developments like People of color Matter, highlight the requirement for resolving well established primary issues.

In Latin America, authentic difficulties, including traditions of dictatorship and common contentions, keep on affecting the basic liberties scene. Issues like native privileges, admittance to equity, and financial disparity stay central focuses. Nations like Venezuela wrestle with political precariousness, prompting worries about community and political freedoms, while others face difficulties connected with the privileges of LGBTQ+ people and orientation based brutality.

Europe:

Europe, with its assorted cluster of countries, faces both normal and locale explicit common freedoms challenges. Western European nations frequently lead with regards to common liberties insurances, however issues like rising xenophobia, hostile to migrant opinion, and difficulties to opportunity of articulation show that no district is invulnerable to misfortunes.

Eastern European countries, molded by post-socialist advances, defy issues like limitations on media opportunity and difficulties to the autonomy of the legal executive. Worries about the freedoms of minorities, including the Roma people group, persevere in specific locales. The European Association assumes a pivotal part in propelling basic liberties through components like the European Court of Common freedoms, adding to a common obligation to maintaining key privileges.

Asia:

The huge and various mainland of Asia epitomizes a range of basic liberties challenges. In East Asia, nations like China wrestle with issues of political restraint, limited opportunity of articulation, and worries about the treatment of ethnic and strict minorities, especially in districts like Xinjiang. The concealment of dispute and common freedoms in Hong Kong has drawn worldwide consideration, stressing the worldwide ramifications of provincial basic liberties issues.

In South Asia, challenges incorporate standing based separation, orientation based savagery, and dangers to opportunity of articulation. India, while maintaining a lively vote based custom, faces tenacious worries about strict prejudice, limitations on common freedoms, and the privileges of underestimated networks.

Southeast Asia fights with issues of dictatorship, limitations on political opportunities, and difficulties connected with work privileges. The Rohingya emergency in Myanmar epitomizes the area's battle with ethnic and strict pressures, prompting mass relocation and common liberties infringement.

Africa:

Africa, a mainland of different societies and chronicles, wrestles with a scope of basic freedoms challenges. While steps have been made in certain areas, others face issues like furnished clashes, political unsteadiness, and difficulties to vote based administration. The effect of frontier heritages is apparent in issues like land privileges and ethnic strains.

Common liberties challenges in Africa length from worries about appointive respectability and press opportunity to issues of youngster work and female genital mutilation. The landmass additionally faces wellbeing related difficulties, with admittance to medical services and reactions to sicknesses like HIV/Helps introducing complex common liberties issues. Basic liberties safeguards across Africa assume a basic part in pushing for equity and responsibility, frequently despite critical misfortune.

Center East:

The Center East, molded by a complicated exchange of international interests and verifiable pressures, faces multi-layered basic liberties challenges. The district wrestles with dictator administration, limitations on opportunity of articulation, and difficulties to the privileges of ladies and minority gatherings. The Israeli-Palestinian clash stays a longstanding wellspring of common freedoms concerns, incorporating issues of relocation, admittance to essential administrations, and the right to self-assurance.

Nations like Saudi Arabia face investigation for their common freedoms records, especially concerning the treatment of dissenters, limitations on ladies' privileges, and issues connected with transient laborers. The effect of outfitted clashes, like in Syria and Yemen, presents intense helpful difficulties, with non military personnel populaces enduring the worst part of the results.

Normal Subjects and Worldwide Interconnectedness:

While every district faces unmistakable difficulties, normal subjects highlight the interconnectedness of basic freedoms issues on a worldwide scale.

Environmental change, for example, influences weak populaces across mainlands, prompting worries about the right to a sound climate, removal, and admittance to assets. The Coronavirus pandemic, a common worldwide test, has featured differences in medical services frameworks, monetary weaknesses, and the significance of safeguarding the right to wellbeing.

Movement is another worldwide worry that rises above territorial limits. The privileges of outcasts and transients are frequently at the front of basic freedoms conversations, with issues of dislodging, admittance to haven, and the treatment of travelers in confinement habitats requesting worldwide consideration and collaboration.

The job of worldwide establishments, for example, the Assembled Countries, in tending to these worldwide difficulties is significant. Deals and shows, including the Widespread Statement of Basic freedoms and the Practical Improvement Objectives, give a typical structure to maintaining common liberties standards. Territorial bodies, similar to the African Association and the European Association, add to a common obligation to basic freedoms inside their particular circles.

Challenges and the Way Forward:

Notwithstanding critical advancement in the worldwide basic freedoms talk, challenges endure. Tyrant inclinations, international contentions, and the disintegration of popularity based standards present dangers to principal freedoms. Separation in view of race, orientation, identity, and different elements keeps on blocking the full acknowledgment of basic liberties for some people and networks.

In tending to these difficulties, it is fundamental to cultivate worldwide collaboration. The guideline of shared liability highlights the requirement for countries and areas to team up in maintaining common liberties norms. Basic liberties tact, support by common society, and worldwide drives that advance inclusivity and correspondence are fundamental parts of the way forward.

A promise to training and mindfulness is likewise basic. Advancing a culture of common liberties requires lawful structures as well as open comprehension and commitment. Engaging people with information about their privileges and empowering deferential discourse can add to a more comprehensive and freedoms situated worldwide society.

1.3 Key Challenges in Ensuring Human Rights

The mission for guaranteeing and maintaining common freedoms internationally is a continuous undertaking full of intricacies, mirroring the multifaceted interaction of political, social, financial, and social elements.

This investigation dives into key difficulties that hinder the acknowledgment of common freedoms, traversing common and political privileges, monetary, social, and social aspects, as well as the overall difficulties that cut across various districts and settings.

1. Tyranny and Disintegration of Vote based Standards:
   One of the preeminent difficulties in guaranteeing basic freedoms
   is the ascent of tyranny and the disintegration of majority rule
   standards in different areas of the planet. Legislatures, both laid
   out majority rules systems and arising powers, face the impulse to
   focus power, shorten common freedoms, and smother disagree. This
   pattern is exemplified by limitations on the right to speak freely
   of discourse, limits on the option to gather, and the sabotaging
   of autonomous legal executive frameworks. The disintegration of
   popularity based standards smothers political opportunities as well
   as has significant ramifications for the security of a wide cluster of
   common liberties.
   Dictator systems frequently target common liberties protectors,
   writers, and common society associations, establishing an environment of dread that hinders promotion and responsibility endeavors.
   The test lies not just in countering these backward patterns inside individual countries yet in addition in encouraging a worldwide
   agreement that unequivocally maintains the standards of a majority
   rules government and basic freedoms.

2. Imbalance and Segregation:
   The tireless worldwide test of imbalance and segregation stays a significant hindrance to the full acknowledgment of common freedoms.
   Financial variations, segregation in view of race, orientation, nationality, and different variables, and primary disparities inside social
   orders make boundaries to the pleasure in key privileges. Minimized
   people group frequently face foundational separation, restricting
   their admittance to training, medical care, work, and equity.
   The intensification of disparity during emergencies, like the Coronavirus pandemic, features the interconnectedness of monetary and
   social freedoms with more extensive common liberties contemplations. Addressing these provokes requires designated strategies to
   decrease imbalance as well as a principal shift in cultural perspectives and designs that propagate separation.

3. Struggle and Philanthropic Emergencies:
   Outfitted clashes and philanthropic emergencies present intense
   difficulties to the security of common liberties. In struggle zones,
   regular folks frequently endure the worst part of savagery, relocation, and denials of basic liberties. The utilization of compound
   weapons, assaults on medical services offices, and the enrollment
   of youngster fighters abuse worldwide helpful regulation, requesting
   pressing worldwide reactions.
   Philanthropic emergencies, whether brought about by struggle,

cataclysmic events, or general wellbeing crises, compound weaknesses and strain assets, prompting infringement of financial, social, and social privileges. Admittance to fundamental administrations, including medical services, schooling, and clean water, becomes compromised, underscoring the interconnectedness of various elements of common freedoms during emergencies.

4. Computerized Privileges and Innovative Difficulties:

In the time of fast mechanical headway, safeguarding computerized privileges represents an original test to the basic liberties structure. Reconnaissance advances, online control, and the control of computerized stages for political purposes encroach on the right to protection, opportunity of articulation, and admittance to data. The advanced gap, inconsistent admittance to innovation, and the utilization of man-made consciousness raise moral worries and further add to variations in the pleasure in basic liberties.

The test lies in laying out powerful lawful systems that defend computerized privileges, guaranteeing that mechanical progressions don't subvert the standards of human pride and individual opportunities. Finding some kind of harmony between outfitting the advantages of innovation and forestalling its abuse for privileges infringement is fundamental for the fate of common liberties insurance.

5. Natural Debasement and Environmental Change:

Natural debasement and the heightening effects of environmental change present a multi-layered challenge to basic freedoms. Removal because of environment related occasions, dangers to one side to a solid climate, and the unbalanced effect on weak networks highlight the multifacetedness of ecological issues with more extensive basic freedoms concerns.

Safeguarding the privileges of native networks, tending to natural shameful acts, and advancing maintainable advancement become basic despite environmental change. Worldwide participation is fundamental to relieve the ecological difficulties that subvert the acknowledgment of financial, social, and social privileges and compound existing imbalances.

6. Absence of Responsibility and Exemption:

An unavoidable test in guaranteeing basic liberties is the absence of responsibility for culprits of denials of basic liberties. Exemption frequently wins in struggle zones, where atrocities and violations against mankind slip through the cracks. The shortfall of responsibility systems for state-supported viciousness, separation, and defilement hampers the foundation of an equitable and freedoms regarding worldwide request.

The Worldwide Crook Court (ICC) and other global councils assume a basic part in tending to exemption, yet challenges in implementation and the hesitance of certain countries to submit to the locale of these foundations thwart their viability. Reinforcing responsibility systems and advancing a culture of responsibility inside countries are crucial stages toward guaranteeing that common liberties violators face ramifications for their activities.

7. **Exile and Relocation Emergencies:**

The situation of displaced people and transients, driven by struggle, oppression, and natural elements, represents a huge test to basic liberties insurance. Issues of dislodging, admittance to shelter, and the treatment of transients in detainment habitats request global consideration and collaboration. The freedoms of evacuees, including the option to look for haven and security from refoulement, frequently face obstructions as countries wrestle with the intricacies of relocation.

The test lies in creating exhaustive and freedoms based movement arrangements, cultivating worldwide collaboration to address the main drivers of dislodging, and maintaining the rule that the privileges of people don't reduce in light of their relocation status.

8. **General Wellbeing Crises:**

General wellbeing crises, like the Coronavirus pandemic, highlight the sensitive harmony between safeguarding general wellbeing and maintaining basic freedoms. Measures taken to check the spread of the infection, remembering lockdowns and limitations for development, should be proportionate and regard individual freedoms. Notwithstanding, the difficulties arise when crisis estimates lead to maltreatments of force, inconsistent admittance to medical services, and the disregard of underestimated networks.

The test is to lay out systems that guarantee a rights-based way to deal with general wellbeing crises, underscoring straightforwardness, responsibility, and the insurance of weak populaces. Adjusting the basic of general wellbeing with deference for common freedoms stays a basic test for legislatures and global bodies the same.

In exploring these key difficulties, an all encompassing and cooperative methodology is fundamental. Reinforcing worldwide organizations, cultivating worldwide collaboration, and enabling common society to advocate for basic freedoms are primary strides toward beating these difficulties. The comprehensiveness of basic freedoms standards, cherished in global settlements and statements, gives a shared view to countries to cooperate in tending to these unpredictable difficulties. It is through supported responsibility, exchange, and aggregate activity that the vision of an existence where common freedoms are generally regarded and safeguarded can be understood.

Chapter 2

International Human Rights Framework

The worldwide common liberties structure is a foundation of worldwide endeavors to secure and advance the innate respect and freedoms of each and every person. Established in a rich history of philosophical, legitimate, and moral establishments, this system has developed to envelop an exhaustive arrangement of standards, settlements, and organizations that guide countries in their obligation to maintaining common freedoms. This investigation dives into the verifiable development, key parts, and difficulties inside the global common freedoms system, featuring its importance in encouraging a reality where equity, uniformity, and human respect win.

Authentic Development:

The underlying foundations of the global basic liberties structure can be followed back to the outcome of The Second Great War, a period set apart by the monstrosities of the Holocaust and an aggregate acknowledgment of the requirement for an all inclusive obligation to common freedoms.

The detestations of the conflict provoked the drafting of the Widespread Statement of Basic freedoms (UDHR) in 1948, a fantastic record that established the groundwork for the worldwide common liberties system.

Imagined by a variety of global delegates and supported by figures, for example, Eleanor Roosevelt, the UDHR intended to lay out a typical norm of common freedoms that rose above public limits. It enunciated a dream where the intrinsic pride and equivalent privileges of all individuals from the human family shaped the groundwork of opportunity, equity, and harmony. The UDHR, despite the fact that non-restricting, set up for the ensuing advancement of restricting deals and shows that would systematize these standards into enforceable global regulation.

The resulting many years saw the elaboration of lawfully restricting instruments, like the Worldwide Agreement on Common and Political Privileges (ICCPR) and the Global Pledge on Financial, Social and Social Freedoms (ICESCR), both embraced in 1966. These pledges, along with different settlements and shows, shaped the Global Bill of Common liberties, an assortment of instruments that illustrated explicit privileges and commitments of states in the domain of basic freedoms.

Key Parts of the Worldwide Basic freedoms System:

Widespread Statement of Basic freedoms (UDHR): The UDHR, frequently alluded to as the "Magna Carta of mankind," stays an essential report inside the global common liberties system. Involving 30 articles, it covers common, political, financial, social, and social freedoms, laying out a far reaching vision of basic liberties that rises above social and public contrasts. The UDHR, however not lawfully restricting, fills in as an ethical compass and a reference point for ensuing deals and shows.

Worldwide Contract on Common and Political Privileges (ICCPR): Embraced in 1966, the ICCPR centers around common and political freedoms, including the right to life, opportunity of articulation, and the right to a fair preliminary. It lays out components, for example, the Basic freedoms Panel to screen the execution of its arrangements by states parties.

Global Agreement on Monetary, Social and Social Freedoms (ICESCR): Additionally embraced in 1966, the ICESCR tends to financial, social, and social privileges, enveloping the option to work, the right to schooling, and the right to a sufficient way of life. It lays out the Panel on Financial, Social and Social Privileges to manage its execution.

Show on the Disposal of All Types of Victimization Ladies (CEDAW): Took on in 1979, CEDAW is a milestone settlement tending to orientation based segregation. It requires the disposal of oppression ladies in all circles of life and lays out a council to survey expresses gatherings' consistence.

Show on the Privileges of the Youngster (CRC): Sanctioned in 1989, the CRC frames the freedoms of kids, underscoring their right to endurance, improvement, and assurance from double-dealing. The Board of trustees on the Privileges of the Kid screens the execution of this show.

Worldwide Show on the Disposal of All Types of Racial Separation (ICERD): Embraced in 1965, ICERD expects to battle racial segregation and advance comprehension among all races. The Council on the End of Racial Segregation regulates its execution.

Show Against Torment and Other Savage, Barbaric, or Debasing Treatment or Discipline (Feline): Embraced in 1984, Feline denies torment and other horrible types of treatment. The Board of trustees Against Torment screens expresses gatherings' consistence.

Worldwide Work Association (ILO) Shows: The ILO sets global work norms through shows and suggestions tending to different parts of work privileges, including opportunity of affiliation, aggregate bartering, and the disposal of youngster work.

Execution and Checking:

The execution of common liberties guidelines depends on states deliberately becoming gatherings to these deals and shows. Upon approval, states expect the commitment to integrate these norms into their homegrown lawful structures and to report occasionally on their consistence to the particular arrangement bodies.

Settlement bodies, contained free specialists, assume a significant part in observing states gatherings' adherence to their commitments. They survey occasional reports put together by states, participate in useful discoursed, issue proposals, and here and there think about individual grumblings. The point is to guarantee responsibility and give a component to review when basic freedoms infringement happen.

The General Occasional Survey (UPR), laid out by the UN Basic liberties Board, is another system that includes the intermittent audit of the common freedoms records of all UN part states. Through a cooperative and valuable cycle, the UPR expects to advance discourse, participation, and the improvement of common liberties circumstances internationally.

Challenges Inside the Worldwide Common freedoms System:

Execution Hole: While the worldwide basic freedoms system gives a powerful establishment, a persevering test lies in the hole between the responsibility made at the global level and the genuine execution of common liberties guidelines at the public level. A few states, because of multiple factors including political will and asset requirements, battle to coordinate and uphold these principles in their homegrown general sets of laws completely.

Selectivity and Twofold Principles: The use of common freedoms norms is once in a while defaced by selectivity and twofold guidelines, where strong states might sidestep responsibility for basic liberties infringement. International contemplations, monetary interests, and power uneven characters among states can prevent the steady utilization of basic liberties standards.

Asset Limitations: The acknowledgment of monetary, social, and social freedoms frequently requires huge monetary assets. Asset limitations, especially in agricultural countries, can obstruct the viable execution of projects and approaches pointed toward satisfying these privileges, like the right to schooling, wellbeing, and a satisfactory way of life.

Social Relativism: The idea of social relativism represents a test to the comprehensiveness of common liberties. Some contend that social variety ought to be considered when deciphering and applying basic liberties principles. Nonetheless, finding some kind of harmony between social responsiveness and the all inclusiveness of basic freedoms stays a complicated errand.

Non-State Entertainers and Innovation: The rising impact of non-state entertainers, including worldwide organizations and non-legislative elements, presents new difficulties. The effect of innovation on protection, opportunity of articulation, and different privileges requires steady transformation and reevaluation of common liberties guidelines to resolve arising issues in the computerized age.

The Way Forward:

Tending to the difficulties inside the worldwide common liberties system requires an aggregate obligation to fortifying the execution, checking, and implementation components. This includes:

Improved Worldwide Participation: Cooperative endeavors among states, global associations, and common society are fundamental for address difficulties on the whole. Global participation can work with asset sharing, specialized help, and the trading of best practices to upgrade the execution of common liberties norms.

Limit Building: Supporting countries in building their ability to successfully carry out and screen common liberties principles is vital. This includes giving specialized help, preparing, and assets to guarantee that states have the instruments and information expected to satisfy their common liberties commitments.

Advancement of Instruction and Mindfulness: Advancing common freedoms training and mindfulness at the nearby, public, and global levels is central. Engaging people with information about their privileges cultivates a culture of regard for human respect and empowers responsibility.

Tending to Underlying Disparities: Handling the main drivers of primary imbalances, separation, and destitution is vital. An extensive methodology that incorporates financial, social, and social privileges with common and political freedoms is fundamental for cultivating a climate where basic liberties can prosper.

Transformation to Arising Difficulties: The worldwide common freedoms system should ceaselessly adjust to address arising difficulties presented by mechanical headways, natural changes, and changes in worldwide power elements. Customary surveys and updates to existing settlements might be important to guarantee their pertinence in a quickly impacting world.

2.1 United Nations and Human Rights

The Unified Countries (UN) fills in as the superior global organization entrusted with cultivating harmony, collaboration, and the security of crucial common freedoms. The many-sided connection between the UN and basic freedoms has developed over many years, set apart by achievements, challenges, and a continuous obligation to propelling the standards framed in the Widespread Statement of Common liberties (UDHR). This investigation dives into the verifiable setting of the UN's commitment with basic liberties, key systems for protecting privileges, and the difficulties and open doors in exploring this perplexing nexus of worldwide obligation.

Authentic Setting:

The outcome of The Second Great War laid the foundation for the foundation of the Unified Countries and its crucial job in advancing and safeguarding basic liberties. The repulsions of the conflict, including the Holocaust and boundless outrages, highlighted the critical requirement for a global obligation to forestalling such monstrosities later on. In 1945, the UN Sanction was taken on, articulating the association's center standards of harmony, security, and the advancement of basic freedoms.

The fundamental second for the global common liberties system happened in 1948 with the reception of the General Announcement of Basic freedoms (UDHR). Drafted by delegates from different social and lawful foundations, the UDHR exemplified a typical vision of the basic privileges intrinsic to every single person, regardless of identity, nationality, or religion. Eleanor Roosevelt, then the Seat of the UN Commission on Common freedoms, assumed a critical part in supporting the UDHR.

Key Components for Defending Common freedoms:

UN Sanction and Basic freedoms Standards: The UN Contract, while not solely a common liberties record, reveres the association's obligation to advancing and empowering regard for common freedoms.

The preface underscores confidence in essential common liberties, the poise and worth of the human individual, and the equivalent privileges of people. These standards structure the moral and legitimate starting point for the UN's commitment with basic liberties.

Common freedoms Chamber (HRC): Laid out in 2006, the HRC is an essential UN body liable for tending to basic liberties issues worldwide. Made out of 47 part states chose by the Overall Gathering, the HRC conducts ordinary meetings to survey basic liberties circumstances, answer crises, and advance topical conversations. Its General Occasional Survey (UPR) component includes a thorough audit of the common liberties records of all UN part states.

UN General Gathering: The Overall Get together fills in as the fundamental deliberative, policymaking, and agent organ of the UN. Its yearly meetings give a stage to part states to examine and embrace goals connected with basic liberties. The Third Board of the Overall Get together spotlights explicitly on friendly, compassionate, and social issues, including common liberties.

UN Security Chamber: The Security Committee, principally entrusted with keeping up with global harmony and security, can address basic freedoms issues when they comprise a danger to worldwide harmony. It can force sanctions, approve peacekeeping missions, and allude circumstances to the Worldwide Lawbreaker Court (ICC) for the indictment of people answerable for gross common liberties infringement.

Worldwide Arrangements and Shows: The UN has been instrumental in the improvement of global common freedoms deals and shows. Arrangements like the Worldwide Contract on Common and Political Privileges (ICCPR), the Global Pledge on Monetary, Social and Social Freedoms (ICESCR), and the Show Against Torment and Other Horrible, Barbaric or Debasing Treatment or Discipline (Feline) lay out legitimately restricting commitments for states parties.

Basic freedoms Arrangements Bodies: Deal bodies, made out of autonomous specialists, screen the execution of explicit common liberties settlements. For instance, the Basic freedoms Board of trustees directs the ICCPR, while the Council on Monetary, Social and Social Privileges screens the ICESCR. These bodies survey state reports, issue suggestions, and participate in productive discoursed to improve consistence.

Global Official courtroom (ICJ): The ICJ, the important legal organ of the UN, has locale to arbitrate lawful questions between states. While its essential center isn't common freedoms, the ICJ might address basic liberties issues in cases connected with state liability regarding universally improper demonstrations.

Exceptional Systems and Rapporteurs: The UN chooses extraordinary rapporteurs, free specialists, and working gatherings to address explicit common liberties issues or topical regions. These systems work under the Basic liberties Committee and assume a critical part in examining, revealing, and exhorting on common freedoms concerns universally.

Difficulties and Open doors:

Security Board's Job and Selectivity: The Security Chamber's job in tending to common liberties stays argumentative, with worries about selectivity and the potential for political contemplations to impact choices. Finding some kind of harmony between keeping up with global harmony and security and maintaining common freedoms requires cautious thought and progressing change endeavors.

Execution Hole: While the UN sets global principles through settlements and shows, the execution of these norms at the public level shifts broadly. Asset requirements, political will, and different variables add to an execution hole, testing the viability of the worldwide basic liberties structure.

Political Elements and Power Awkward nature: The political elements and power lopsided characteristics among UN part states frequently influence the association's capacity to reliably address basic freedoms infringement. Strong states might apply impact, and international contemplations can block the fair-minded requirement of basic liberties standards.

Social Relativism and Power Concerns: The guideline of social relativism, where social contrasts are viewed as in the translation and use of common liberties principles, brings up issues about the comprehensiveness of freedoms. Power concerns might lead a few states to oppose global mediation in their homegrown undertakings, convoluting endeavors to address basic freedoms infringement.

Asset Requirements: The UN faces asset imperatives that cutoff its ability to really address the multi-layered nature of common liberties challenges. Satisfactory financing, institutional help, and participation among part states are vital for upgrading the UN's capacity to satisfy its common freedoms order.

Arising Issues in the Computerized Age: The quick headway of innovation acquaints new difficulties with basic liberties, including concerns connected with advanced security, observation, and opportunity of articulation on the web. The UN should adjust its structures to resolve these arising issues and guarantee that common freedoms are safeguarded in the advanced age.

Collaboration with Non-State Entertainers: Actually tending to common freedoms challenges requires participation with non-state entertainers, including common society associations, organizations, and grassroots developments. Building organizations and connecting with assorted partners are fundamental for far reaching and practical common liberties drives.

2.2 Treaties and Conventions

Settlements and shows are the foundations of the worldwide common freedoms system, giving a lawful establishment to the insurance and advancement of central privileges across the globe. These lawfully authoritative arrangements, arranged and took on by countries, lay out a typical arrangement of guidelines that rise above boundaries and societies. This investigation dives into the meaning of arrangements and shows in propelling common freedoms, their verifiable development, key instruments, and the difficulties and accomplishments in their execution.

Verifiable Development:

The verifiable development of basic freedoms arrangements and shows can be followed back to the consequence of The Second Great War and the drafting of the Widespread Announcement of Common liberties (UDHR) in 1948. The UDHR, however not lawfully restricting, laid the basis for ensuing deals that systematized explicit privileges and commitments. The last part of the 1950s and 1960s saw the reception of two fundamental pledges: the Worldwide Contract on Common and Political Privileges (ICCPR) and the Global Agreement on Financial, Social and Social Freedoms (ICESCR), the two of which came into force in 1976.

These pledges shaped piece of the Global Bill of Basic liberties, close by the UDHR, on the whole addressing a thorough system that enveloped common, political, monetary, social, and social freedoms. Throughout the long term, the global local area proceeded to refine and grow this structure, bringing about a bunch of deals and shows that address explicit privileges, weak gatherings, and arising issues.

Key Instruments:

Global Pledge on Common and Political Privileges (ICCPR):

Taken on in 1966, the ICCPR centers around common and political privileges, including the right to life, opportunity of articulation, and the right to a fair preliminary. It lays out the Common liberties Panel, which surveys state reports and issues suggestions to guarantee consistence with the pledge.

Global Agreement on Financial, Social and Social Freedoms (ICESCR):

Taken on close by the ICCPR in 1966, the ICESCR tends to financial, social, and social privileges, including the option to work, the right to schooling, and the right to a sufficient way of life. The Board on Monetary, Social and Social Freedoms screens its execution.

Show Against Torment and Other Horrible, Brutal or Corrupting Treatment or Discipline (Feline):

Taken on in 1984, Feline precludes torment and other awful types of treatment. The Panel Against Torment audits express gatherings' consistence, conducts requests, and addresses individual objections.

Show on the End of All Types of Victimization Ladies (CEDAW):

Ordered in 1979, CEDAW is a milestone settlement tending to orientation based separation. It requires the disposal of oppression ladies in all circles of life and lays out the Board of trustees on the End of Victimization Ladies to screen consistence.

Show on the Freedoms of the Kid (CRC):

Taken on in 1989, the CRC frames the privileges of youngsters, underlining their right to endurance, improvement, and security from double-dealing. The Panel on the Privileges of the Youngster screens its execution and audits state reports.

Global Show on the End of All Types of Racial Separation (ICERD):

Taken on in 1965, ICERD means to battle racial segregation and advance comprehension among all races. The Council on the Disposal of Racial Segregation manages its execution and analyzes state reports.

Global Work Association (ILO) Shows:

The ILO sets global work guidelines through shows and suggestions tending to different parts of work privileges, including opportunity of affiliation, aggregate bartering, and the disposal of kid work.

These instruments, among others, on the whole comprise a thorough structure for the security and advancement of common freedoms, mirroring the variety and reliance of privileges across various circles of life.

Importance and Accomplishments:

The meaning of settlements and shows in the domain of common liberties is multi-layered. These instruments give a typical language and set of rules that rise above social, political, and lawful contrasts, cultivating a common obligation to maintaining human pride. They lay out a lawful system that empowers responsibility, guaranteeing that states are considered liable for satisfying their commitments and that people have roads for looking for change for privileges infringement.

Additionally, settlements and shows add to the advancement of global standard regulation by classifying developing standards and guidelines. They act as impetuses for lawful and strategy changes at the public level, provoking states to adjust their homegrown regulation to worldwide basic liberties commitments. The revealing components laid out by deal bodies empower peer survey, working with the trading of best practices and empowering states to gain from one another's triumphs and difficulties.

The accomplishments of basic freedoms settlements and shows are apparent in various regions. For instance, the ICCPR and ICESCR play played significant parts in propelling the acknowledgment and security of common and political freedoms, as well as financial, social, and social privileges, separately. The CRC has added to expanded mindfulness and activity for the freedoms of youngsters, affecting public regulation, strategies, and projects pointed toward protecting their prosperity.

Deals, for example, CEDAW have been instrumental in tending to orientation based separation, encouraging a worldwide comprehension of ladies' freedoms and provoking legitimate changes to propel orientation correspondence. The Show on the Privileges of People with Handicaps (CRPD), took on in 2006, addresses a huge move toward perceiving and guaranteeing the freedoms of people with incapacities, advancing inclusivity and openness.

Difficulties and Limits:

In spite of their importance, basic liberties arrangements and shows face difficulties and restrictions that influence their adequacy:

Execution Hole: The interpretation of worldwide commitments into substantial enhancements at the public level frequently experiences difficulties. Asset limitations, absence of political will, and contending needs block the viable execution of basic liberties principles.

Selectivity and Lopsided Consistence: States may specifically consent to specific commitments while dismissing others, prompting lopsided consistence across the common freedoms range. International contemplations and power lopsided characteristics among states can impact the prioritization of specific privileges over others.

Asset and Limit Requirements: Settlement bodies, entrusted with observing consistence, may confront asset and limit imperatives. The volume of state reports to be assessed, the intricacy of issues, and the requirement for mastery in different regions can strain the viability of these bodies.

Restricted Requirement Components: While deals lay out commitments, the implementation instruments accessible are in many cases restricted. The shortfall of a unified implementation authority requires dependence on state consistence, which might be impacted by political contemplations.

Social Relativism and Sway Concerns: Discussions encompassing social relativism and worries about power keep on testing the all inclusiveness of common freedoms. A few states contend that specific privileges might be deciphered and applied contrastingly founded on social settings, convoluting endeavors to lay out predictable principles.

Arising Issues and Mechanical Difficulties: Fast innovative progressions present new basic freedoms challenges, like advanced protection, reconnaissance, and the effect of man-made consciousness. Guaranteeing that deals stay pertinent notwithstanding developing innovations requires progressing transformation and understanding.

The Way Forward:

To address these difficulties and influence the maximum capacity of basic liberties deals and shows, a few systems can be sought after:

Improved Execution and Consistence Components: Reinforcing instruments for the execution and it is crucial for screen of common freedoms deals. This incorporates tending to asset imperatives, upgrading announcing processes, and giving specialized help to states in satisfying their commitments.

Advancement of Training and Mindfulness: Bringing issues to light about basic liberties deals among states, common society, and the overall population is significant. Training projects can enable people to declare their freedoms, while mindfulness missions can encourage a culture of regard for human respect.

Resolving Arising Issues: Consolidating arrangements in existing settlements to address arising common freedoms challenges, especially in the computerized domain, is fundamental. This might include adjusting current arrangements or growing new instruments that explicitly address the ramifications of innovative headways on basic liberties.

Reinforcing Global Participation: Improved collaboration among states, worldwide associations, and common society is indispensable for really tending to cross-line basic freedoms challenges. Cooperative endeavors can prompt the sharing of best practices, assets, and skill.

Propelling Responsibility: Advancing responsibility for basic liberties infringement requires tending to exemption, reinforcing public and worldwide legal instruments, and guaranteeing that people answerable for gross infringement are considered to be responsible.

2.3 Role of International Organizations

Worldwide associations assume an essential part in the worldwide work to protect and advance basic freedoms. These associations, spreading over local and worldwide substances, act as discussions for discourse, participation, and the improvement of techniques to address complex common liberties challenges. This investigation dives into the complex job of global associations in maintaining common freedoms, analyzing their verifiable development, key capabilities, and the difficulties they face in exploring the unique scene of basic liberties security.

Verifiable Development:

The job of global associations in basic liberties assurance has advanced essentially over the course of the last hundred years. The Class of Countries, laid out in 1920 after The Second Great War, was the forerunner to the Assembled Countries (UN) and one of the earliest efforts to encourage worldwide collaboration. In any case, the Association confronted limits, especially in forestalling the flare-up of The Second Great War and tending to boundless denials of basic freedoms.

In the fallout of The Second Great War, the Unified Countries was established in 1945 with a focal obligation to keeping up with global harmony and security. The UN Contract explained rules that laid the preparation for the assurance of basic freedoms, accentuating the nobility and worth of the human individual. The resulting many years saw the foundation of particular offices inside the UN, like the Assembled Countries Instructive, Logical and Social Association (UNESCO) and the Global Work Association (ILO), which added to the improvement of standards and principles connected with common liberties.

Provincial associations, including the European Association (EU), the African Association (AU), and the Association of American States (OAS), likewise arose as critical entertainers in advancing and safeguarding basic liberties inside their separate locales. These associations supplement the worldwide endeavors of the UN and give fitted ways to deal with address provincial difficulties and specificities.

Key Elements of Global Associations:

Standardizing Improvement:

Global associations add to the improvement of worldwide standards and norms connected with basic freedoms. Through shows, settlements, and announcements, these elements lay out a typical system that guides part states in their obligation to maintaining major freedoms.

The Widespread Statement of Common freedoms (UDHR), took on by the UN General Gathering in 1948, remains as an essential report that has impacted resulting global settlements.

Checking and Announcing:

Worldwide associations assume a basic part in observing the common freedoms circumstance in part states. This includes exploring state reports, directing examinations, and giving proposals to address common liberties infringement. Deal bodies, like the UN Basic liberties Board and its Exceptional Strategies, as well as provincial bodies like the European Court of Common freedoms, give systems to responsibility and oversight.

Limit Building and Specialized Help:

Perceiving the different limits of part states, worldwide associations take part in limit building drives and give specialized help to improve the execution of basic liberties principles. This includes supporting legitimate changes, preparing policing legal authorities, and encouraging institutional systems that advance common liberties inside countries.

Compromise and Peacekeeping:

Global associations, especially the UN, take part in compromise and peacekeeping endeavors to address circumstances where basic freedoms are under danger. Peacekeeping missions might incorporate the security of regular people, checking truces, and supporting the foundation of stable administration structures that regard common liberties.

Backing and Mindfulness:

Worldwide associations act as promoters for basic freedoms on the worldwide stage. They bring issues to light about unambiguous issues, prepare general assessment, and attempt to make a feeling of divided liability between part states. Through missions, reports, and public proclamations, these associations add to molding a worldwide talk on common freedoms.

Legitimate Review and Equity:

Global associations give roads to legitimate change and equity in instances of basic liberties infringement. The Global Lawbreaker Court (ICC), laid out in 2002, prosecutes people for destruction, violations against humankind, atrocities, and the wrongdoing of animosity. Provincial courts, like the Between American Court of Basic liberties, additionally mediate common freedoms cases inside their purviews.

Coordination and Participation:

The coordination and participation of global associations are fundamental for tending to diverse basic freedoms challenges. Joint drives, data sharing, and cooperative endeavors empower a more extensive and compelling reaction to issues, for example, exile emergencies, illegal exploitation, and pandemics.

Challenges in Exploring the Basic freedoms Scene:

Political Limitations and Power Concerns:

The sway of states and political contemplations frequently present difficulties to the powerful working of global associations in the domain of common freedoms. A few states might oppose outside examination or mediation in their inner undertakings, making snags to checking and implementation endeavors.

Asset Requirements:

Numerous worldwide associations face asset imperatives that limit their ability to address the huge range of common freedoms challenges. Satisfactory financing, staffing, and calculated help are pivotal for these substances to really satisfy their orders.

Selectivity and Irregularity:

The selectivity and irregularity in the utilization of common freedoms guidelines by worldwide associations can dissolve their validity. International contemplations and power elements among part states might impact navigation, prompting lopsided reactions to basic freedoms infringement.

Restricted Requirement Components:

While worldwide associations add to the advancement of basic liberties standards, their requirement systems are much of the time restricted. The shortfall of an incorporated implementation authority requires dependence on state consistence and willful participation, which might be impacted by political contemplations.

Intricacy of Diverse Issues:

Common freedoms challenges frequently meet with other complex issues, like equipped struggles, neediness, and ecological emergencies. Resolving these diverse issues requires a planned and coordinated approach among worldwide associations, which might confront difficulties in adjusting their methodologies and needs.

Arising Issues and Mechanical Difficulties:

Quick innovative progressions present new basic liberties challenges, like advanced protection, observation, and the effect of man-made consciousness. Global associations should adjust to these arising issues, yet their customary systems may not be appropriate to address the intricacies of the advanced age.

Absence of General Participation:

A few global associations, especially territorial bodies, may need general enrollment, prompting holes in inclusion and security. The viability of these associations might be compromised when certain states decide not to take part or are prohibited from enrollment.

The Way Forward:

To explore the difficulties and keep propelling common liberties, worldwide associations can think about the accompanying methodologies:

Fortifying Responsibility Components:

Upgrading responsibility components inside worldwide associations is fundamental. This incorporates advancing straightforwardness, tending to irreconcilable circumstances, and laying out strong components to consider part states responsible for basic freedoms infringement.

Advancing Comprehensiveness and Inclusivity:

Endeavors ought to be made to advance the all inclusiveness of basic liberties and guarantee the inclusivity of worldwide associations. Empowering all states to take part and effectively participate in basic freedoms drives cultivates a more extensive and delegate approach.

Embracing Mechanical Development:

Worldwide associations should adjust to innovative headways by integrating advanced freedoms contemplations into their structures. This includes resolving issues like internet based protection, computerized observation, and the moral utilization of arising advancements.

Improving Participation and Coordination:

Cooperative endeavors among worldwide associations are fundamental for tending to complex common liberties challenges. Fortifying coordination components, sharing data, and encouraging a feeling of collaboration can prompt more powerful reactions to complex issues.

Enabling Common Society:

Global associations ought to effectively draw in with and enable common society associations, which assume a urgent part in observing basic freedoms, pushing for responsibility, and enhancing the voices of minimized networks.

Tending to Main drivers:

To actually address basic freedoms challenges, worldwide associations ought to pursue tending to main drivers, including destitution, imbalance, and separation. A comprehensive methodology that coordinates basic liberties into more extensive turn of events and it is fundamental to peacebuilding techniques.

Advancing Preventive Strategy:

Accentuating preventive tact can assist worldwide associations with tending to common freedoms issues before they grow into emergencies. Early intercession and intervention endeavors can add to the avoidance of contention and denials of basic freedoms.

Chapter 3

National Responses to Human Rights

Public reactions to common liberties challenges are vital to the security and advancement of essential opportunities inside the boundaries of individual states. As sovereign substances, countries assume a basic part in maintaining the privileges and poise of their residents. This investigation digs into the multi-layered scene of public reactions to basic freedoms, looking at the authentic development, key components, difficulties, and valuable open doors inside the setting of homegrown endeavors to defend and propel common liberties.

Authentic Development:

The authentic development of public reactions to common liberties is unpredictably associated with more extensive social, political, and financial changes. The acknowledgment of common liberties at the public level acquired unmistakable quality in the outcome of The Second Great War, as the revulsions of the Holocaust and different barbarities provoked a worldwide obligation to forestalling such maltreatments later on. This responsibility tracked down articulation in the Widespread Statement of Basic liberties (UDHR) in 1948, a record that put forward a typical norm of freedoms to be delighted in by all individuals.

In the many years that followed, countries progressively coordinated basic freedoms standards into their constitutions, lawful systems, and arrangements. The foundation of worldwide common freedoms deals and shows gave an establishment to states to adjust their homegrown regulations to worldwide principles. The Worldwide Bill of Basic liberties, included the UDHR, the Global Contract on Common and Political Freedoms (ICCPR), and the Global Pledge on Monetary, Social and Social Privileges (ICESCR), turned into a foundation for molding public reactions to basic liberties challenges.

Key Components inside Public Reactions:

Established Securities:

Numerous countries insert common freedoms assurances straight-forwardly into their constitutions. Established arrangements act as a key system for defending individual freedoms and giving a premise to lawful difficulties to privileges infringement. Constitutions frequently count key privileges, like opportunity of articulation, the right to a fair preliminary, and insurances against segregation.

Public Basic freedoms Organizations (NHRIs):

Public Basic freedoms Organizations assume a vital part in checking, advancing, and safeguarding common liberties inside individual nations. These free bodies are frequently entrusted with researching protests of privileges infringement, exhorting legislatures on basic liberties consistence, and raising public mindfulness. Successful NHRIs add to building a culture of regard for basic liberties at the public level.

Authoritative Systems:

Public councils order regulations that give impact to worldwide common liberties principles. Regulation covering regions like law enforcement, hostile to segregation, and work freedoms mirrors a country's obligation to maintaining common liberties standards. Parliamentary oversight and commitment are basic in guaranteeing that homegrown regulations line up with global commitments.

Legal Instruments:

The legal executive assumes an essential part in deciphering and up-holding common freedoms securities. Public courts settle cases including claimed freedoms infringement, giving a critical road to people to look for change. Legal choices add to the improvement of legitimate points of reference that shape the comprehension and use of basic freedoms inside a particular general set of laws.

Common Society Commitment:

Common society associations, including non-administrative associa-tions (NGOs), support gatherings, and grassroots developments, assume a fundamental part in observing basic liberties, bringing issues to light, and considering legislatures responsible. Their commitment frequently includes giving an account of freedoms infringement, pushing for lawful changes, and offering help to impacted networks.

Training and Mindfulness Projects:

Legislatures put resources into schooling and mindfulness projects to advance a culture of common liberties inside their social orders. These drives expect to engage residents with information about their privileges, encourage resistance and inclusivity, and challenge prejudicial perspec-tives. Instructive endeavors add to the drawn out objective of building a basic liberties cognizant populace.

Worldwide Participation:

Public reactions to basic freedoms challenges frequently include joint effort with the worldwide local area. States partake in worldwide discussions, participate in discretionary drives, and add to worldwide endeavors pointed toward tending to transnational basic liberties issues. Collaboration with worldwide associations and adherence to settlement commitments mirror a promise to the interconnected idea of basic freedoms.

Challenges in Public Reactions:

Execution Hole:

Notwithstanding legitimate systems and established securities, there is much of the time a hole between the acknowledgment of common liberties in principle and their powerful execution practically speaking. Asset requirements, institutional shortcomings, and deficient political will can ruin the interpretation of legitimate certifications into substantial upgrades in the existences of people.

Particular Execution and Implementation:

A few countries may specifically execute and uphold basic freedoms insurances, stressing specific privileges while dismissing others. This specific methodology might be impacted by political contemplations, social perspectives, or authentic heritages, prompting irregularities in the assurance of privileges across various gatherings or issues.

Absence of Admittance to Equity:

In numerous nations, hindrances to getting to equity continue, restricting people's capacity to look for change for basic liberties infringement. Factors like financial inconsistencies, restricted legitimate guide, and terrorizing may hinder the successful activity of lawful cures, especially for underestimated or weak populaces.

Political Obstruction and Dictatorship:

Political obstruction and dictator administration present huge difficulties to common freedoms. Now and again, legislatures abridge common freedoms, smother disagree, and sabotage the autonomy of the legal executive and different establishments. Tyrant systems might utilize oppressive measures to keep up with control, prompting inescapable denials of basic freedoms.

Segregation and Minimization:

Segregation in view of variables like race, orientation, identity, religion, or sexual direction keeps on being an unavoidable test. Minimized people group frequently face foundational hindrances that limit their admittance to training, medical services, and monetary open doors, sustaining patterns of imbalance and freedoms infringement.

Outfitted Struggle and Security Concerns:

Countries wrestling with outfitted struggle or security concerns might confront difficulties in adjusting the assurance of common freedoms with the basic to keep up with dependability. Crisis estimates taken during clashes might prompt freedoms misuses, and endeavors to battle psychological oppression now and again bring about the disintegration of common freedoms.

Social Relativism and Conventional Practices:

Social relativism, where social practices are viewed as in the translation of basic liberties, can be a quarrelsome issue. Some contend that social customs ought to be regarded, while others affirm that specific practices might disregard all around perceived common liberties norms. Offsetting social responsiveness with the security of individual privileges stays a mind boggling task.

Open doors for Development:

Reinforcing Public Common freedoms Foundations:

Putting resources into the autonomy and adequacy of Public Common freedoms Establishments can improve their ability to address privileges infringement. Guaranteeing that NHRIs have satisfactory assets, lawful power, and public trust is urgent for their part in advancing common freedoms locally.

Advancing Regulative Changes:

Countries can focus on regulative changes to adjust homegrown regulations to global common liberties guidelines. Tending to holes in legitimate systems, revoking unfair regulations, and establishing regulation that safeguards the freedoms of underestimated bunches add to an additional powerful basic liberties climate.

Engaging Common Society:

State run administrations can establish an empowering climate for common society associations to work openly and add to basic freedoms backing. Safeguarding the freedoms of activists, columnists, and NGOs encourages an energetic common society that can play a guard dog job and consider specialists responsible.

Training and Sharpening Efforts:

Legislatures can put resources into thorough schooling and mindfulness missions to advance a culture of common liberties. Integrating basic freedoms training into school educational plans, directing public mindfulness programs, and drawing in with news sources add to building a rights-cognizant society.

Worldwide Coordinated effort and Friend Audit:

Taking part in worldwide gatherings and teaming up with different countries can give chances to peer survey and common learning. Sharing prescribed procedures, taking part in strategic drives, and sticking to worldwide basic freedoms components add to a worldwide culture of regard for common liberties.

Tending to Underlying drivers of Disparity:

Endeavors to address the underlying drivers of disparity, segregation, and minimization are fundamental. Legislatures can execute strategies that advance financial and social consideration, destroy foundational boundaries, and engage underestimated networks to take part completely in the public arena.

Struggle Avoidance and Goal:

Proactive measures to forestall clashes and resolve existing debates can add to the security of common liberties. Political endeavors, peace-building drives, and adherence to global philanthropic regulation during outfitted clashes are basic for alleviating the effect of savagery on non military personnel populaces.

3.1 Diversity in National Approaches

Variety in public ways to deal with basic freedoms highlights the intricacy of exploring the complex woven artwork of legitimate, social, and political scenes across the globe. While the widespread standards cherished in worldwide basic liberties instruments give a typical establishment, the translation and execution of these standards change fundamentally among countries. This investigation digs into the complex elements of variety in public ways to deal with common liberties, looking at the variables that impact unique ways, the difficulties presented by such variety, and the open doors it presents for cultivating a more comprehensive and nuanced comprehension of basic freedoms.

Factors Affecting Variety:

Social and Verifiable Setting:

The social and verifiable setting of every country shapes its way to deal with basic liberties. Social qualities, customs, and verifiable encounters impact how social orders see individual freedoms, shared prosperity, and the job of the state. Varieties in legitimate customs, for example, custom-based regulation versus common regulation frameworks, add to disparate understandings and uses of common freedoms standards.

Political Frameworks and Administration:

The political frameworks and administration designs of countries assume a crucial part in molding their common freedoms draws near. Vote based and tyrant systems frequently show particular ways to deal with common freedoms, opportunity of articulation, and law and order. In popular governments, there might be more noteworthy accentuation on individual freedoms and responsibility, while dictator systems might focus on dependability and state control.

Legitimate Structures and Sacred Insurances:

The legitimate structures and sacred insurances inside countries act as significant determinants of their basic freedoms rehearses. Countries with powerful protected arrangements unequivocally defending basic freedoms might move toward issues uniquely in contrast to those without such express assurances. The presence of established courts and the degree to which global basic liberties standards are integrated into home-grown regulation further add to variety.

Financial and Social Setting:

The financial and social setting of a country impacts its capacity to satisfy specific common liberties commitments. Financial variables, like neediness, imbalance, and admittance to instruction and medical services, can affect the acknowledgment of monetary, social, and social privileges. Countries confronting asset requirements might focus on advancement objectives in an unexpected way, prompting varieties in the execution of freedoms.

International Contemplations:

International contemplations and local elements add to variety in public ways to deal with common freedoms. Nations confronting explicit security challenges or local contentions might embrace estimates that could be seen as encroaching on individual freedoms in light of a legitimate concern for public safety. Territorial associations, like the European Association, may impact basic liberties rehearses inside their part states.

Public Perspectives and Cultural Assumptions:

Public perspectives and cultural assumptions about basic freedoms assume an essential part in forming public methodologies.

Social mentalities toward issues like orientation correspondence, LGBTQ+ privileges, and opportunity of articulation can differ generally, impacting the regulative and strategy scene. Legislatures might adjust their approaches to winning accepted practices or, now and again, challenge existing standards through legitimate changes.

Worldwide Relations and Discretion:

The worldwide relations and political contemplations of countries likewise influence their basic freedoms draws near. Nations might tailor their common liberties way of talking and strategies in view of conciliatory relations, worldwide partnerships, and the craving to extend a specific picture on the global stage. This can bring about varieties in how countries draw in with global basic liberties systems.

Challenges Presented by Variety:

Irregularities in Privileges Assurance:

Variety in public methodologies can prompt irregularities in the security of common liberties. While certain countries might focus on specific freedoms, others might accord less significance to them. This dissimilarity makes difficulties in accomplishing a predictable worldwide norm for common liberties, as understandings fluctuate generally.

Specific Utilization of Freedoms:

The specific utilization of freedoms is a repetitive test. Countries might focus on specific privileges while dismissing others, prompting lopsided characteristics in the assurance of common, political, monetary, social, and social freedoms. This particular methodology might be impacted by social, political, or authentic contemplations.

Challenges in Worldwide Participation:

Various public methodologies can present difficulties to worldwide collaboration on basic freedoms issues. Variations in values, lawful practices, and needs might block cooperative endeavors to address transnational difficulties, for example, environmental change, movement, or pandemics, from a basic liberties point of view.

Potential for Freedoms Misuses:

Dissimilar methodologies make the potential for denials of basic freedoms, particularly when countries focus on solidness, security, or monetary advancement over individual freedoms. Tyrant systems might take advantage of the absence of worldwide agreement to smother disagree, diminish opportunities, and execute basic liberties infringement without risk of punishment.

Restricted Responsibility Systems:

The absence of predictable principles and standards hampers responsibility instruments. Without any all around settled upon standards, implementation components might be lacking to really address basic freedoms infringement. This can prompt circumstances where states sidestep responsibility for freedoms manhandles.

Social Relativism Discussions:

Variety in approaches frequently ignites banters around social relativism. The pressure among comprehensiveness and social particularity brings up issues about whether certain freedoms ought to be dependent upon social understandings, possibly subverting the all inclusiveness of common liberties.

Security versus Freedoms Situation:

Countries confronting security difficulties might wrestle with the situation of offsetting safety efforts with the assurance of individual privileges. Crisis estimates taken during clashes or emergencies might encroach upon privileges, bringing up moral issues about the OK furthest reaches of state intercession.

Open doors for Encouraging Inclusivity:

Discoursed and Multifaceted Comprehension:

Making spaces for open exchanges and encouraging culturally diverse comprehension can advance inclusivity. Worldwide gatherings, scholarly trades, and social discretion drives work with discussions that recognize and regard assorted points of view on common freedoms.

Limit Building and Specialized Help:

Supporting countries in limit assembling and giving specialized help can connect holes in the execution of basic freedoms norms. Cooperative endeavors to share best practices, offer preparation programs, and give assets add to an additional sound and powerful worldwide common liberties structure.

Advancing Comprehensiveness Through Training:

Schooling assumes a key part in advancing the comprehensiveness of basic freedoms. Endeavors to coordinate basic liberties training into school educational programs, bring issues to light about worldwide norms, and draw in with neighborhood networks add to building a common perspective of principal freedoms.

Fortifying Worldwide Collaboration:

Reinforcing worldwide participation is fundamental for tending to worldwide difficulties. Cooperative endeavors among countries, local associations, and worldwide bodies can defeat dissimilar methodologies and encourage an aggregate obligation to maintaining common freedoms standards.

Advancing Common Society Commitment:

Common society associations act as basic entertainers in advancing inclusivity. Engaging common society through security of their privileges, cultivating an empowering climate for activism, and giving stages to minimized voices add to an additional comprehensive basic freedoms talk.

Empowering Companion Survey Instruments:

Peer audit instruments inside global associations and provincial bodies give potential open doors to countries to gain from one another's encounters. Helpful criticism and sharing of best practices add to a ceaseless course of progress in basic liberties rehearses.

Adjusting Social Awareness and All inclusiveness:

Finding some kind of harmony between social awareness and all inclusiveness is fundamental. Perceiving the significance of social setting while at the same time maintaining center basic freedoms standards considers a more nuanced and comprehensive methodology that regards different social points of view.

3.2 Legal Frameworks and Protections

Lawful systems and insurances structure the foundation of endeavors to shield basic freedoms at both public and worldwide levels. These structures include a scope of regulations, settlements, and establishments intended to explain, secure, and uphold the crucial privileges and opportunities intrinsic to all people. This investigation dives into the unpredictable scene of lawful systems and securities, looking at their authentic development, the job of global settlements, the foundation of public establishments, and the difficulties and open doors inborn in their execution.

Verifiable Development:

The verifiable development of legitimate systems and insurances for basic liberties follows a way from early philosophical ideas to present day worldwide instruments. The post-The Second Great War period saw an essential second with the reception of the General Statement of Basic liberties (UDHR) in 1948. Created in light of the monstrosities of the conflict, the UDHR spread out a thorough arrangement of privileges that are inborn to all people, regardless of identity, nationality, or different qualities.

The UDHR, while non-restricting, set up for resulting worldwide arrangements that would convey lawful weight. The Global Agreement on Common and Political Privileges (ICCPR) and the Worldwide Contract on Monetary, Social and Social Freedoms (ICESCR), both embraced in 1966, are among the basic deals that along with the UDHR comprise the Global Bill of Common liberties. These settlements laid out legitimately restricting commitments on states to regard, secure, and satisfy a wide cluster of privileges, going from the right to life and opportunity of articulation to one side to work and partake in a satisfactory way of life.

Job of Worldwide Deals:

Worldwide settlements act as basic instruments for laying out worldwide principles and standards for common freedoms. Confirmation of these deals means a state's obligation to maintaining and carrying out the freedoms revered inside them. Past the ICCPR and ICESCR, various different settlements center around unambiguous parts of common liberties, like the Show on the Disposal of All Types of Oppression Ladies (CEDAW), the Show on the Freedoms of the Youngster (CRC), and the Show Against Torment and Other Brutal, Cruel or Corrupting Treatment or Discipline (Feline).

Deal bodies, made out of free specialists, screen state consistence with these settlements. States parties submit occasional reports enumerating their endeavors to execute the settlement arrangements, and the deal bodies give valuable input and suggestions. This checking system adds to the responsibility of states in satisfying their common liberties commitments.

The Discretionary Convention to the ICCPR and different systems permit people to submit objections to worldwide bodies when their privileges have been abused locally and all suitable cures have been depleted. These instruments broaden the span of basic liberties assurances past public lines, empowering people to look for change at the worldwide level.

Public Foundations:

At the public level, the foundation of establishments devoted to basic freedoms assumes a urgent part in guaranteeing the viable execution of lawful structures. Public Basic liberties Establishments (NHRIs) act as free bodies entrusted with checking, advancing, and safeguarding basic freedoms inside their separate nations. The Paris Standards, took on in 1991, give rules to the foundation and working of these establishments, accentuating variables like autonomy, pluralism, and adequacy.

NHRIs embrace a scope of capabilities, including exploring basic freedoms infringement, directing exploration, giving instruction and mindfulness, and exhorting legislatures on common liberties strategies. Their job is especially crucial in cultivating a culture of regard for common freedoms at the homegrown level. Nations, incorporating those with a hearty lawful system, benefit from the presence of NHRIs as extra shields to guarantee the privileges of people are maintained.

Past NHRIs, the legal framework assumes a significant part in the security of common liberties. Public courts settle cases including affirmed infringement of freedoms, decipher protected arrangements in accordance with global principles, and add to the advancement of legitimate points of reference. The rule of legal survey engages courts to evaluate the defendability of regulations and government activities, going about as a mind possible maltreatments of force.

Difficulties and Open doors in Execution:

While legitimate systems and securities are fundamental, their viable execution faces a scope of difficulties. These difficulties, nonetheless, likewise present open doors for refinement and improvement chasing more strong common freedoms security.

Particular Execution and Authorization:

One outstanding test is the particular execution and requirement of common freedoms. States might focus on specific freedoms over others, and political contemplations now and then lead to conflicting application. This selectivity represents a gamble of ignoring specific weak gatherings or issues.

Opportunity: Tending to this challenge includes advancing a far reaching and incorporated way to deal with basic liberties. Drives that underscore the indissoluble nature and relationship of privileges can encourage a more all encompassing comprehension and use of common liberties standards.

Asset Requirements:

Numerous countries face asset requirements that influence their capacity to execute common liberties securities completely. Restricted subsidizing, staffing, and framework can obstruct the foundation of viable components for observing, detailing, and review.

Opportunity: Worldwide participation and help assume a vital part in tending to asset imperatives. Cooperative endeavors, limit building drives, and specialized help projects can uphold countries in upgrading their common freedoms foundation.

Political Obstruction:

Political obstruction represents a test to the freedom and viability of public organizations liable for common liberties. Legislatures might try to impact or subvert crafted by these establishments to keep away from responsibility for freedoms infringement.

Opportunity: Fortifying the freedom of NHRIs and the legal executive requires a pledge to the standards of law and order and partition of abilities. Global strain, discretionary commitment, and common society promotion can add to relieving political impedance.

Social Responsiveness and Relativism:

Offsetting social responsiveness with the comprehensiveness of common liberties stays a mind boggling task. Banters around social relativism frequently emerge, addressing whether certain privileges ought to be dependent upon social understandings.

Opportunity: Advancing social awareness while maintaining all inclusive standards includes cultivating open exchanges and understanding. Common freedoms training and mindfulness missions can add to dissipating social relativism legends and elevating a common obligation to essential privileges.

Restrictions of Worldwide Systems:

Global components, while urgent, face restrictions in their capacity to uphold basic freedoms principles. The shortfall of a brought together requirement authority and the dependence on state consistence make difficulties in considering people and states responsible for infringement.

Opportunity: Reinforcing worldwide components includes investigating roads for upgrading implementation systems. Engaging worldwide bodies, like the Worldwide Lawbreaker Court, and elevating adherence to worldwide legitimate commitments add to an additional powerful worldwide basic liberties structure.

Arising Basic liberties Difficulties:

Fast mechanical headways, ecological emergencies, and new types of contention present arising difficulties to common liberties that may not be satisfactorily tended to by existing lawful structures.

Opportunity: Adjusting lawful structures to address arising difficulties requires adaptability and prescience. States, global associations, and common society can team up to foster new standards and principles that address the ramifications of innovative headways, environmental change, and developing clash elements.

Common Society Commitment:

The job of common society is fundamental in the security and advancement of basic freedoms. Be that as it may, common society associations frequently face limitations, badgering, and terrorizing, restricting their capacity to actually contribute.

Opportunity: Enabling common society includes supporting for the assurance of their privileges, establishing an empowering climate for their exercises, and participating in discretionary endeavors to address limitations on common society.

3.3 Challenges in Implementing Human Rights at the National Level

The execution of common liberties at the public level is a multi-layered try that includes deciphering legitimate structures and global responsibilities into substantial enhancements in the existences of people. While huge headway has been made in articulating worldwide norms for common freedoms, the difficulties in actually understanding these privileges at the public level are assorted and complex. This investigation dives into the multifaceted scene of difficulties, looking at issues like political elements, institutional deficiencies, financial variables, social contemplations, and the job of common society in exploring the complicated excursion of basic liberties execution.

Political Elements and Administration Difficulties:

Political Will and Prioritization:

One of the premier difficulties in carrying out common freedoms at the public level is the differing level of political will among state run administrations. The obligation to common liberties can be affected by political needs, for certain legislatures focusing on solidness, monetary turn of events, or security over privileges insurance. This absence of political will can appear in lacking distribution of assets, hesitance to authorize vital legitimate changes, and restricted endeavors to address fundamental common freedoms issues.

Tending to the Test: Encouraging political will includes support, mindfulness missions, and commitment with political pioneers. Common society, worldwide associations, and discretionary endeavors can assume a significant part in advancing the combination of basic freedoms into public plans.

Tyranny and Restraint:

Countries with tyrant systems represent a one of a kind arrangement of difficulties to common liberties execution. In such settings, states might limit opportunity of articulation, stifle disagree, and shorten common freedoms for the purpose of keeping up with control. The absence of majority rule foundations and balanced governance can compound denials of basic freedoms.

Tending to the Test: Global tension, political intercessions, and designated approvals can be techniques to address dictatorship. Engaging common society to oppose suppression, reporting basic liberties infringement, and using worldwide systems for responsibility are critical in testing dictator rehearses.

Institutional Shortcomings and Defilement:

Institutional shortcomings, including defilement inside government bodies and the legal executive, can sabotage endeavors to carry out common liberties. Debasement dissolves law and order, obstructs admittance to equity, and cultivates a climate where denials of basic liberties can continue unrestrained.

Tending to the Test: Fortifying organizations requires hostile to debasement measures, legal changes, and the foundation of free oversight instruments. Global help for limit building drives and straightforwardness endeavors can add to tending to institutional shortcomings.

Financial Variables and Disparity:

Destitution and Financial Inconsistencies:

Destitution and financial inconsistencies present critical difficulties to the acknowledgment of monetary, social, and social freedoms. Admittance to schooling, medical services, lodging, and business can be compromised in financially distraught networks, sustaining patterns of destitution and imbalance.

Tending to the Test: Battling neediness includes executing social approaches, financial changes, and designated programs that address the main drivers of disparity. A rights-based way to deal with improvement underscores the significance of guaranteeing that monetary strategies focus on the prosperity, everything being equal.

Separation and Underestimation:

Separation in light of variables like race, orientation, identity, religion, or sexual direction stays an unavoidable test. Underestimated people group frequently face foundational obstructions that limit their admittance to open doors and administrations, prompting common liberties infringement.

Tending to the Test: Dispensing with segregation requires lawful changes, mindfulness missions, and governmental policy regarding minorities in society measures. Comprehensive strategies that address the particular requirements of underestimated bunches add to cultivating a more impartial society.

Admittance to Training and Data:

Restricted admittance to training and data is a hindrance to the acknowledgment of common liberties. Without training, people might know nothing about their privileges, incapable to advocate for themselves, and powerless to abuse and segregation.

Tending to the Test: Advancing schooling and data dispersal includes putting resources into instruction foundation, guaranteeing admittance to quality training for all, and using media and correspondence channels to bring issues to light about common liberties.

Social Contemplations and Conventional Practices:

Social Relativism and Orientation Balance:

Social relativism can present difficulties to the execution of basic freedoms, especially according to orientation fairness. A few social practices might propagate orientation based separation, limiting the privileges and chances of ladies and young ladies.

Tending to the Test: Offsetting social responsiveness with the advancement of orientation balance includes drawing in networks in discoursed, testing unsafe standards, and encouraging a rights-based approach that regards social variety while maintaining widespread standards.

Native Privileges and Land Questions:

Native people group frequently face difficulties in the security of their freedoms, especially with respect to land and asset debates. Abuse, removal, and absence of acknowledgment of native freedoms can prompt basic liberties infringement.

Tending to the Test: Regarding native freedoms includes legitimate acknowledgment of land possession, significant conference in dynamic cycles, and tending to the financial variations looked by native networks.

Job of Common Society and Difficulties to Activism:

Limitations on Common Society:

Common society associations (CSOs) assume a significant part in supporting for basic freedoms. Nonetheless, in certain nations, legislatures force limitations on CSOs, restricting their capacity to work openly, voice concerns, and promoter for freedoms.

Tending to the Test: Guarding the space for common society includes worldwide promotion, discretionary strain, and cooperative endeavors to safeguard the freedoms of activists. Reinforcing nearby polite society flexibility through preparing and limit building drives is fundamental.

Dangers to Basic freedoms Safeguards:

Basic freedoms safeguards frequently face dangers, provocation, and savagery for their activism. Legislatures, strong vested parties, and non-state entertainers might target people supporting for privileges, establishing an unfriendly climate for activism.

Tending to the Test: Safeguarding basic freedoms protectors requires legitimate systems for their wellbeing, worldwide fortitude, and endeavors to consider culprits responsible. Worldwide associations and discretionary channels can offer help and perceivability for safeguards in danger.

Absence of Legitimate Cures and Responsibility:

In numerous specific circumstances, the absence of viable legitimate cures and responsibility systems represents a critical test. People might confront snags in looking for review for basic liberties infringement, prompting a culture of exemption.

Tending to the Test: Fortifying lawful cures includes legitimate changes, laying out free oversight systems, and improving admittance to equity. Global bodies, for example, the Worldwide Crook Court, assume a part in holding culprits of serious common liberties infringement responsible.

Chapter 4

Non-Governmental Organizations (NGOs) and Human Rights

Non-Legislative Associations (NGOs) assume a critical part in propelling the reason for common freedoms on a worldwide scale. These associations, driven by standards of equity, correspondence, and compassion, work freely of government designs and influence their impact to address common liberties infringement, advocate for strategy changes, and offer help to underestimated networks. This investigation digs into the multilayered job of NGOs in the domain of common liberties, looking at their authentic development, various capabilities, challenges confronted, and the effect they have on forming the talk and practice of basic freedoms around the world.

Verifiable Development:

The verifiable development of NGOs in the common liberties field is intently attached to more extensive developments for civil rights and the journey to shield people from maltreatments of force.

The outcome of The Second Great War, with the foundation of the Unified Countries and the reception of the General Statement of Basic liberties in 1948, denoted a defining moment. NGOs tracked down a stage to add to the worldwide exchange on common liberties inside the system of the recently shaped global organizations.

The rise of NGOs as key entertainers picked up speed during the decolonization period and the social liberties developments of the 1950s and 1960s. Grassroots associations, like the Southern Christian Authority Gathering and the American Common Freedoms Association in the US, became pioneers in pushing for social liberties. At the same time, worldwide NGOs like Absolution Global (established in 1961) and Basic liberties Watch (established in 1978) started to zero in on checking denials of basic freedoms universally and advancing responsibility.

The finish of the Virus War additionally catalyzed the development of NGOs into new locales, tending to a wide range of privileges, including common and political freedoms, financial and social privileges, and social freedoms. NGOs assumed a urgent part in preparing popular assessment, impacting global strategies, and considering legislatures responsible for common freedoms infringement.

Various Elements of NGOs in Basic freedoms:

Checking and Announcing:

NGOs effectively take part in checking basic freedoms conditions around the world. Through hands on work, exploration, and documentation, they focus on occasions of misuse, segregation, and viciousness. Reports distributed by NGOs act as significant assets for policymakers, the media, and general society, revealing insight into underreported issues and considering culprits responsible.

Promotion and Strategy Impact:

NGOs advocate for strategy changes at neighborhood, public, and worldwide levels. They draw in with states, worldwide associations, and different partners to impact regulation, challenge prejudicial practices, and advance the reception of common liberties well disposed arrangements. Their support endeavors add to the production of legitimate structures that line up with worldwide basic liberties norms.

Lawful Help and Portrayal:

NGOs frequently give lawful help to people and networks confronting common freedoms infringement. This might include supporting casualties in legal actions, recording claims against culprits, or mediating as amicus curiae in huge legal disputes. Lawful help guarantees admittance to equity for the individuals who may somehow or another be underestimated or hushed.

Limit Building and Schooling:

NGOs participate in limit building drives to engage networks and nearby associations. Studios, preparing programs, and instructive missions center around bringing issues to light about basic liberties, cultivating metro interest, and furnishing people with the information to advocate for their freedoms.

Crisis Reaction and Helpful Guide:

During emergencies like equipped struggles, cataclysmic events, or general wellbeing crises, NGOs frequently assume a vital part in giving helpful guide. This incorporates conveying food, clinical help, safe house, and insurance administrations to impacted populaces. Basic liberties contemplations are vital to their crisis reaction endeavors.

Local area Strengthening and Grassroots Drives:

NGOs work at the grassroots level to enable underestimated networks. Through people group based projects, they address financial imbalances, advance orientation uniformity, and backing drives that upgrade the general prosperity of weak populaces. Engaging people group is viewed as a manageable way to deal with common liberties insurance.

Global Backing Efforts:

NGOs influence their worldwide organizations and impact to direct global backing efforts. Issues, for example, environment equity, exile freedoms, and the annulment of the death penalty have been the focal point of inescapable missions that plan to collect open help, prepare assets, and strain legislatures to make a move.

Challenges Looked by NGOs:

Financing Requirements:

Numerous NGOs face monetary difficulties, depending on gifts, gives, and raising support endeavors to support their tasks. The capriciousness of financing streams can impede long haul arranging and effect the congruity of fundamental common freedoms work.

Tending to the Test: Differentiating subsidizing sources, building vital organizations, and pushing for supported monetary help from state run administrations and confidential benefactors are methodologies to relieve financing requirements.

Political Impedance and Suppression:

NGOs, particularly those functioning in areas with dictator systems, may confront political obstruction, badgering, and suppression. States might force prohibitive regulations, keep an eye on activists, or mark associations as dangers to public safety, restricting their capacity to unreservedly work.

Tending to the Test: Worldwide fortitude, strategic strain, and lawful backing are pivotal in testing political impedance. Organizing with similar associations and using worldwide components for assurance add to flexibility against constraint.

Security Dangers and Dangers:

Common freedoms safeguards and NGO staff frequently face individual security gambles. Dangers, terrorizing, and savagery coordinated at people dealing with on delicate problems or in struggle zones present critical difficulties to the security of those supporting for common freedoms.

Tending to the Test: Executing strong safety efforts, giving preparation on wellbeing conventions, and laying out networks for crisis reaction are fundamental parts of tending to security chances.

Intricacy of Worldwide Issues:

Tending to complicated, interconnected worldwide issues, for example, environmental change, constrained movement, and transnational denials of basic freedoms requires coordination and joint effort across borders. The sheer scale and intricacy of these difficulties can strain the assets and limits of individual NGOs.

Tending to the Test: Cooperative drives, organizations, and alliances empower NGOs to pool assets, share ability, and altogether tackle diverse worldwide difficulties.

Authenticity and Responsibility:

Guaranteeing the authenticity and responsibility of NGOs is fundamental for keeping up with public trust. Worries about straightforwardness, administration, and moral lead might emerge, especially as NGOs participate in high-stakes backing and mediation.

Tending to the Test: Carrying out powerful inside administration structures, sticking to moral principles, and embracing straightforwardness in monetary and functional issues add to building and keeping up with authenticity.

Discontinuity and Contest:

The multiplication of NGOs figuring out on comparable problems can prompt discontinuity and rivalry for assets. Coordination difficulties might emerge, impeding the viability of aggregate endeavors.

Tending to the Test: Building organizations, cultivating cooperation, and decisively separating subject matters can assist with resolving issues of discontinuity and improve the effect of aggregate drives.

Effect and Future Bearings:

The effect of NGOs on the scene of basic freedoms is certain. Their work has added to huge progressions, including the foundation of worldwide legitimate structures, the arrival of political detainees, the cancelation of unfair regulations, and the mindfulness raising on basic common liberties issues. NGOs have been instrumental in molding public talk, impacting strategies, and considering states responsible for their common freedoms commitments.

Looking forward, the job of NGOs in basic freedoms is probably going to develop in light of arising difficulties and valuable open doors. The advanced age presents new roads for backing, empowering NGOs to use innovation for correspondence, preparation, and documentation. Issues like computerized freedoms, algorithmic inclination, and the convergence of innovation and common liberties are progressively becoming central focuses for NGOs.

In addition, the developing acknowledgment of the interconnectedness of basic freedoms with other worldwide difficulties, including natural manageability, monetary equity, and general wellbeing, highlights the requirement for NGOs to embrace comprehensive methodologies that address the main drivers of privileges infringement. Cooperative endeavors that span areas and disciplines will be critical in exploring the intricacies of the contemporary basic liberties scene.

4.1 Role and Impact of NGOs

Non-Legislative Associations (NGOs) have become crucial entertainers in the contemporary worldwide scene, employing huge impact in different areas like basic freedoms, advancement, ecological protection, and general wellbeing. The multi-layered job of NGOs rises above geological limits, and their effect is significant in molding arrangements, pushing for minimized networks, and encouraging positive change. This investigation digs into the dynamic and developing job of NGOs, looking at their capabilities, influence, challenges confronted, and the expected roads for future commitments in a quickly impacting world.

Elements of NGOs:

Support and Strategy Impact:

A focal capability of NGOs is support, including endeavors to impact strategies and dynamic cycles at neighborhood, public, and worldwide levels. NGOs act as voices for minimized networks, utilizing their ability to advocate for strategy changes that line up with standards of equity, uniformity, and common freedoms. Through research, campaigning, and key correspondence, NGOs assume a urgent part in molding lawful systems and institutional practices.

Administration Arrangement and Local area Strengthening:

Numerous NGOs are participated in direct help arrangement, tending to the prompt necessities of networks in regions like medical services, schooling, and philanthropic guide. Past this, NGOs frequently embrace an all encompassing methodology that underlines local area strengthening. By working straightforwardly with networks, NGOs look to construct neighborhood limits, upgrade independence, and address the main drivers of social issues.

Checking and Detailing:

NGOs take part in orderly checking of basic freedoms infringement, ecological corruption, and different types of foul play. This includes hands on work, exploration, and documentation of cases where privileges are encroached upon or where fundamental issues continue. Through nitty gritty reports and distributions, NGOs bring issues to light, assemble public help, and add to the responsibility of people and foundations answerable for infringement.

Limit Building and Schooling:

NGOs assume an imperative part in limit building, giving preparation and schooling to people and networks. This incorporates basic freedoms instruction, expertise improvement, and mindfulness crusades. Engaging people with information and abilities improves their capacity to advocate for their freedoms, partake in dynamic cycles, and add to economical turn of events.

Crisis Reaction and Compassionate Guide:

In the midst of emergencies, including furnished clashes, cataclysmic events, and general wellbeing crises, NGOs are frequently at the very front of giving philanthropic guide. This includes conveying prompt help like food, haven, and clinical help to impacted populaces. NGOs additionally add to the drawn out recuperation and reproduction endeavors as a team with different partners.

Legitimate Help and Portrayal:

NGOs habitually offer lawful help to people and networks confronting denials of basic freedoms. This incorporates lawful portrayal, promotion in court, and backing for casualties looking for change. Legitimate intercessions by NGOs add to the authorization of privileges and the advancement of admittance to equity, particularly for minimized or weak gatherings.

Examination and Development:

NGOs add to investigate drives that create information and bits of knowledge into squeezing social issues. This exploration frequently illuminates strategy proposals, program improvement, and promotion techniques. NGOs likewise assume a part in cultivating development, investigating new ways to deal with address complex difficulties, and directing drives that can be increased for more extensive effect.

Effect of NGOs:

Affecting Strategies and Lawful Systems:

Maybe one of the main effects of NGOs is their part in affecting strategies and lawful structures. Through proof based backing, commitment with leaders, and assembly of general assessment, NGOs add to the detailing and correction of regulations and strategies that better reflect common liberties standards and civil rights.

Advancing Responsibility and Straightforwardness:

NGOs assume a significant part in holding legislatures, enterprises, and other strong substances responsible for their activities. By uncovering denials of basic freedoms, natural infringement, and degenerate practices, NGOs add to straightforwardness and responsibility. Their guard dog capability guarantees that those liable for bad behavior are considered responsible, encouraging a culture of liability and moral direct.

Enabling Minimized People group:

NGOs working at the grassroots level enable minimized networks by giving them devices, assets, and information. Through people group driven drives, NGOs add to the strengthening of people, encouraging a feeling of organization and self-assurance. This strengthening is vital to breaking patterns of destitution, segregation, and social prohibition.

Catalyzing Social Change:

NGOs frequently act as impetuses for social change, testing cultural standards, biased rehearses, and foundational imbalances. Their backing endeavors add to moving public mentalities, bringing issues to light, and testing instilled biases. Whether resolving issues of orientation equity, LGBTQ+ privileges, or racial equity, NGOs assume an extraordinary part in reshaping cultural stories.

Tending to Worldwide Difficulties:

NGOs are instrumental in tending to complex worldwide difficulties, for example, environmental change, relocation, and general wellbeing emergencies. Through worldwide joint effort, cross-sectoral organizations, and inventive methodologies, NGOs add to tracking down answers for these interconnected difficulties. Their deftness and capacity to work across borders make them fundamental entertainers chasing after worldwide prosperity.

Giving a Voice to the Voiceless:

One of the central jobs of NGOs is intensifying the voices of the people who are underestimated, persecuted, or quieted. By giving a stage to people and networks to share their encounters, NGOs guarantee that these accounts are heard on the worldwide stage. This intensification is an integral asset for testing shamefulness and pushing for significant change.

Filling Holes in Help Arrangement:

NGOs frequently work in regions where taxpayer supported organizations might be deficient or blocked off. By filling holes in assistance arrangement, especially in medical care, schooling, and social administrations, NGOs add to worked on prosperity and personal satisfaction for networks. Their intercessions supplement government endeavors and address explicit necessities that could somehow be disregarded.

Challenges Looked by NGOs:

Financing Limitations and Reliance:

A steady test for some NGOs is getting supportable financing. Dependence on awards, gifts, and raising support endeavors can make monetary vulnerability, affecting the progression and size of their projects. A few NGOs face difficulties in expanding subsidizing sources, prompting a level of reliance on a set number of benefactors.

Tending to the Test: NGOs can moderate subsidizing imperatives by embracing different raising money methodologies, building associations with magnanimous associations, and investigating creative funding models. Long haul arranging and monetary supportability ought to be fundamental parts of authoritative systems.

Political Impedance and Restraint:

NGOs, particularly those functioning in areas with tyrant systems, may confront political impedance, badgering, and suppression. Legislatures might institute prohibitive regulations, keep an eye on activists, or name associations as dangers to public safety, restricting their capacity to uninhibitedly work.

Tending to the Test: Conquering political obstruction includes building unions, framing alliances, and participating in essential support at both public and global levels. NGOs can use political tension, draw in with common freedoms components, and utilize legitimate roads to challenge harsh measures.

Security Dangers and Dangers:

Basic liberties safeguards and NGO staff frequently face individual security chances. Dangers, terrorizing, and brutality coordinated at people taking care of on delicate problems or in struggle zones present huge difficulties to the security of those upholding for common freedoms.

Tending to the Test: Executing powerful safety efforts, giving preparation on wellbeing conventions, and laying out networks for crisis reaction are fundamental parts of tending to security chances. Worldwide fortitude and backing components likewise assume a part in safeguarding people in danger.

Intricacy of Worldwide Issues:

Tending to perplexing, interconnected worldwide issues, for example, environmental change, constrained movement, and transnational denials of basic liberties requires coordination and cooperation across borders. The sheer scale and intricacy of these difficulties can strain the assets and limits of individual NGOs.

Tending to the Test: Cooperative drives, organizations, and alliances empower NGOs to pool assets, share mastery, and aggregately tackle multi-layered worldwide difficulties. Key unions with state run administrations, organizations, and scholarly foundations can improve the effect of NGO intercessions.

Authenticity and Responsibility Concerns:

Guaranteeing the authenticity and responsibility of NGOs is fundamental for keeping up with public trust. Worries about straightforwardness, administration, and moral direct may emerge, especially as NGOs take part in high-stakes promotion and mediation.

Tending to the Test: NGOs can improve authenticity by taking on straightforward works on, sticking to moral norms, and effectively captivating with partners. Inner administration structures that focus on responsibility and receptiveness add to building and keeping up with trust.

Fracture and Rivalry:

The expansion of NGOs figuring out on comparative problems can prompt discontinuity and contest for assets. Coordination difficulties might emerge, frustrating the viability of aggregate endeavors.

Tending to the Test: Building organizations, encouraging joint effort, and decisively separating subject matters can assist with resolving issues of discontinuity and improve the effect of aggregate drives. Stages for information sharing and coordination can work with more powerful co-operation.

Future Roads for NGOs:

Advanced Development and Innovation:

Embracing computerized development and innovation is a vital road for NGOs to improve their effect. The utilization of information investigation, web-based entertainment, and computerized stages can enhance backing endeavors, work with correspondence, and assemble public help. Embracing mechanical progressions additionally opens additional opportunities for effective program execution and observing.

Multifacetedness and Comprehensive Methodologies:

Perceiving the multifacetedness of basic liberties issues and taking on comprehensive methodologies is fundamental for tending to complex difficulties. NGOs can pursue incorporating their intercessions across areas, taking into account the interconnected idea of issues like neediness, disparity, and ecological corruption.

Local area Driven and Participatory Methodologies:

Reinforcing people group driven and participatory methodologies guarantees that the voices and needs of networks are at the very front of NGO intercessions. Enabling people group to effectively take part in dynamic cycles encourages maintainability, nearby possession, and social pertinence in programs.

Promotion for Fundamental Change:

NGOs can progressively zero in on upholding for foundational change by tending to underlying drivers of shamefulness and imbalance. This includes testing primary issues, prejudicial approaches, and institutional practices that propagate denials of basic liberties. Upholding for fundamental change adds to long haul, manageable effect.

Putting resources into Limit Building and Authority Advancement:

Focusing on limit building and administration advancement inside NGOs reinforces hierarchical strength. Putting resources into the expert improvement of staff, cultivating authority abilities, and advancing variety inside administration structures add to authoritative viability and flexibility.

Worldwide Fortitude and Systems administration:

Building worldwide fortitude and reinforcing networks among NGOs make a strong power for change. Joint effort on a worldwide scale empowers NGOs to share assets, skill, and best practices. Joint drives, composed missions, and aggregate backing endeavors can enhance the effect of NGOs in tending to worldwide difficulties.

Schooling and Mindfulness Missions:

NGOs can keep on assuming a urgent part in schooling and mindfulness crusades. By utilizing their skill, organizations, and stages, NGOs can teach general society on squeezing basic liberties issues, cultivate compassion, and prepare support for positive social change. Schooling stays an amazing asset for molding public mentalities and impacting strategy choices.

4.2 Successful NGO Initiatives

Non-Legislative Associations (NGOs) have been instrumental in starting and executing fruitful undertakings that address a wide exhibit of social, monetary, and ecological difficulties.

These drives, driven by a pledge to positive change, epitomize the extraordinary effect NGOs can have on networks and social orders. This investigation digs into the attributes and results of fruitful NGO drives, featuring key models across various areas and districts.

Attributes of Fruitful NGO Drives:

Local area Driven Approach:

Fruitful NGO drives are in many cases established locally driven approach, where the requirements, goals, and voices of the local area are focused on. This approach includes dynamic commitment with local area individuals, grasping their unique circumstance, and cooperatively planning mediations that line up with neighborhood needs. Drives that engage networks to take responsibility for will quite often be more manageable and significant in the long haul.

All encompassing and Incorporated Arrangements:

Numerous fruitful NGO drives embrace an all encompassing and coordinated way to deal with critical thinking. Perceiving the interconnectedness of social issues, these drives address various features of an issue instead of handling secluded side effects. For instance, a wellbeing centered drive could likewise think about training, financial open doors, and natural variables to make an extensive and maintainable effect.

Associations and Coordinated efforts:

Building key organizations and coordinated efforts is a typical trait of fruitful NGO drives. NGOs frequently work with states, different NGOs, neighborhood organizations, scholastic foundations, and local area pioneers to pool assets, aptitude, and organizations. Cooperative endeavors empower a more thorough reaction to complex difficulties and upgrade the versatility and replicability of fruitful models.

Advancement and Flexibility:

Effective NGO drives exhibit a limit with respect to development and versatility. NGOs frequently influence new advances, inventive systems, and proof based practices to address arising difficulties. The capacity to adjust to evolving conditions, gain from encounters, and consolidate criticism upgrades the adequacy of drives and guarantees significance in powerful conditions.

Strengthening and Limit Building:

Engaging people and networks lies at the core of numerous effective NGO drives. Whether through schooling, ability improvement, or administration preparing, these drives try to fabricate the limit of local area individuals to effectively take part in dynamic cycles and become problem solvers. Enabled people group are stronger and better prepared to support positive results.

Information Driven Direction:

Effective NGO drives frequently depend on information driven dynamic cycles. Gathering and dissecting pertinent information assists NGOs with grasping the effect of their mediations, distinguish regions for development, and arrive at informed conclusions about asset portion. This proof based approach improves responsibility and straightforwardness in project execution.

Support for Strategy Change:

Numerous effective NGO drives expand their effect past direct intercessions by pushing for strategy changes. By drawing in with policymakers, leading exploration, and utilizing public help, NGOs add to the production of an empowering climate that upholds positive social change. Backing endeavors guarantee that the effect of fruitful drives is supported and increased at a fundamental level.

Instances of Effective NGO Drives:

Grameen Bank (Bangladesh):

Established by Muhammad Yunus in 1983, the Grameen Bank spearheaded the idea of microfinance, giving little credits to ruined people, especially ladies, to begin or extend private companies. This drive enabled ladies in provincial Bangladesh, breaking the pattern of destitution and advancing financial independence. The outcome of the Grameen Bank model has propelled comparable microfinance drives around the world, exhibiting the extraordinary force of monetary consideration.

BRAC's Schooling Project (Worldwide):

BRAC, initially known as Bangladesh Provincial Progression Council, has carried out a fruitful training program that arrives at a great many youngsters in Asia and Africa. The program centers around giving quality instruction, particularly to young ladies and minimized networks. By utilizing imaginative showing techniques, local area commitment, and an all encompassing methodology that addresses financial hindrances, BRAC has taken critical steps in further developing training results in districts with restricted admittance to quality schooling.

Greenpeace's Ecological Missions (Worldwide):

Greenpeace, a worldwide ecological association, has been at the front of fruitful missions to resolve worldwide natural issues. Their drives frequently include direct activity, support, and raising public mindfulness. Models incorporate missions against atomic testing, deforestation, and environmental change. Greenpeace's effect reaches out past prompt mediations, affecting general assessment, molding strategy plans, and considering companies and state run administrations responsible for their natural practices.

Medecins Sans Frontieres (Specialists Without Lines) - Medical care in Struggle Zones (Worldwide):

Medecins Sans Frontieres (MSF) has been a trailblazer in giving medical services in struggle zones and regions impacted by helpful emergencies. Through its decentralized and adaptable methodology, MSF conveys crisis clinical consideration where it is generally required. By exploring perplexing and testing conditions, MSF has saved endless lives and featured the critical requirement for supported medical services in districts confronting savagery, uprooting, and flimsiness.

Kiva's Microfinance Stage (Worldwide):

Kiva, a non-benefit association, has fostered a fruitful web-based stage that associates loan specialists with business people needing microloans. Kiva's model permits people all over the planet to contribute limited quantities of cash to help organizations in low-pay areas. This drive advances monetary consideration, enables business visionaries, and makes a worldwide local area participated in supportable financial turn of events.

Space to Peruse - Proficiency and Young ladies' Schooling (Worldwide):

Space to Peruse centers around further developing proficiency and orientation fairness in training, with a specific accentuation on young ladies' strengthening. Through its projects, including school development, libraries, and young ladies' schooling drives, Space to Peruse has emphatically influenced huge number of kids across Asia and Africa. The association's comprehensive methodology tends to hindrances to instruction, advancing a culture of perusing and learning.

Oxfam's Maintainable Occupation Projects (Different Nations):
Oxfam, a worldwide confederation of NGOs, has carried out fruitful feasible occupation programs in different nations. These drives address destitution and disparity by supporting networks in creating feasible farming, getting to business sectors, and building strength to environmental change. Oxfam's incorporated methodology perceives the interconnected idea of social and financial difficulties, going for the gold at both neighborhood and fundamental levels.

Difficulties and Examples Learned:
While fruitful NGO drives have accomplished excellent results, they are not without challenges. Normal difficulties include:

Manageability:
Keeping up with the manageability of positive results past the underlying period of a drive can challenge. Guaranteeing that networks have the assets, abilities, and frameworks set up to proceed with the advancement accomplished is essential for long haul achievement.

Scale and Replicability:
Scaling effective drives to arrive at bigger populaces and reproducing them in various settings present difficulties. Factors like social contrasts, differing financial circumstances, and the requirement for versatility can affect the adaptability and replicability of effective models.

Reliance on Outer Financing:
Numerous fruitful NGO drives are reliant upon outer sources of financial support, making them defenseless against variances in subsidizing accessibility. Expanding subsidizing streams and investigating reasonable monetary models are fundamental for the life span of fruitful drives.

Estimating Effect:
Precisely estimating and evaluating the effect of a drive can be complicated. The complex idea of social issues frequently requires nuanced pointers and subjective evaluations. Creating vigorous checking and assessment structures is fundamental for grasping the genuine effect of drives.

Political and Administrative Difficulties:
NGOs might confront political and administrative difficulties, particularly while working in districts with prohibitive administration structures. Exploring political scenes, building unions, and upholding for an empowering climate are fundamental for beating these difficulties.

Social Responsiveness:
Understanding and regarding neighborhood societies is basic for the outcome of drives. Absence of social awareness can prompt obstruction from networks and block the viability of intercessions. Fruitful drives focus on social setting and local area support in program plan.

Adjusting to Dynamic Conditions:

Social, financial, and natural settings are dynamic, expecting drives to adjust to evolving conditions. The capacity to explore vulnerabilities, gain from encounters, and change techniques in like manner adds to supported achievement.

4.3 Challenges Faced by NGOs

Non-Legislative Associations (NGOs) assume a fundamental part in tending to squeezing worldwide difficulties, supporting for basic freedoms, and driving positive change. Notwithstanding, the scene where NGOs work is full of intricacies and difficulties that can altogether influence their adequacy. This investigation digs into the diverse difficulties looked by NGOs, enveloping monetary limitations, political elements, security chances, authenticity concerns, and the always developing worldwide setting.

Monetary Imperatives:

One of the most unavoidable difficulties looked by NGOs is monetary imperatives. Numerous NGOs depend on a blend of awards, gifts, and raising support endeavors to support their tasks. Nonetheless, the flightiness of subsidizing streams, benefactor needs, and rivalry for assets can make monetary precariousness. This challenge is especially articulated for more modest or grassroots associations that might miss the mark on monetary stores to climate variances in financing.

Tending to this challenge includes enhancing subsidizing sources, investigating imaginative supporting models, and building practical associations. NGOs need to foster vigorous raising money techniques, develop associations with various givers, and put resources into long haul monetary wanting to upgrade their monetary versatility.

Political Impedance and Suppression:

NGOs, particularly those working in locales with dictator systems, frequently face political obstruction and suppression. Legislatures might institute prohibitive regulations, force administrative obstacles, or transparently go against the exercises of NGOs saw as rocking the boat. Political impedance can appear as legitimate limitations, reconnaissance of activists, and endeavors to smother opportunity of articulation and gathering.

Defeating political impedance requires key commitment at both public and worldwide levels. NGOs can construct collusions with similar associations, take part in conciliatory support, and influence global common liberties components to apply strain on legislatures that obstruct their work. Exploring the fragile harmony among support and government relations is significant for supporting effect.

Security Dangers and Dangers:

Basic liberties protectors and NGO staff frequently work in testing and once in a while risky conditions, presenting them to individual security gambles. Dangers, terrorizing, and viciousness coordinated at people figuring out on delicate problems or in struggle zones present huge difficulties to the wellbeing of those supporting for common freedoms.

Alleviating security chances includes carrying out strong safety efforts, giving preparation on wellbeing conventions, and laying out networks for crisis reaction. Global fortitude and backing systems are fundamental parts of safeguarding people in danger. NGOs may likewise team up with nearby networks and specialists to improve the security of their work force.

Intricacy of Worldwide Issues:

NGOs frequently wrestle with the intricacy of interconnected worldwide issues, for example, environmental change, constrained movement, and transnational denials of basic freedoms.

Tending to these multi-layered difficulties requires coordination, joint effort, and a comprehension of the different variables at play. The sheer scale and intricacy of these issues can strain the assets and limits of individual NGOs.

To explore the intricacy of worldwide issues, NGOs ought to focus on cooperation and association building. Taking part in alliances, organizations, and cooperative drives empowers NGOs to pool assets, share aptitude, and on the whole tackle difficulties that surpass the limit of any single association. Taking on an interdisciplinary methodology and it is additionally essential to remain informed about arising patterns.

Authenticity and Responsibility Concerns:

Guaranteeing the authenticity and responsibility of NGOs is fundamental for keeping up with public trust and validity. Worries about straightforwardness, administration, and moral direct may emerge, especially as NGOs participate in high-stakes support and mediation. Issues connected with the abuse or bungle of assets can additionally affect an association's standing.

NGOs can address authenticity and responsibility worries by executing hearty interior administration structures, sticking to moral guidelines, and embracing straightforwardness in monetary and functional issues. Open correspondence with partners, including givers, recipients, and the more extensive public, is indispensable for building and keeping up with trust.

Fracture and Rivalry:

The expansion of NGOs dealing with on comparative problems can prompt discontinuity and contest for assets. Coordination difficulties might emerge, obstructing the adequacy of aggregate endeavors. Absence of coordinated effort can bring about duplicative exercises, wasteful asset portion, and decreased influence.

Tending to fracture and contest includes building organizations, encouraging cooperation, and decisively separating subject matters. NGOs can profit from sharing data, assets, and best practices inside the area, at last upgrading the effect of aggregate drives. Stages for information sharing and coordination can work with more compelling cooperation.

Legitimate and Administrative Difficulties:

NGOs frequently face legitimate and administrative difficulties that change across locales. A few states force prohibitive regulations that limit the space for common society, including prerequisites for enrollment, detailing, and exposure. Lawful obstacles can block the capacity of NGOs to work openly and successfully.

To explore legitimate and administrative difficulties, NGOs need to remain informed about neighborhood regulations, participate in lawful promotion, and look for global help while confronting unreasonable limitations.

Building collusions with legitimate specialists, common liberties associations, and neighborhood advocates upgrades the limit of NGOs to successfully answer lawful difficulties.

Public Discernment and Deception:

NGOs might experience difficulties connected with public discernment and deception. Errors about the idea of their work, philosophical inclinations, or purposeful falsehood missions can impact general assessment and effect an association's capacity to assemble support.

NGOs can address this test by proactively drawing in with people in general, giving precise data about their exercises, and developing a straightforward and open correspondence technique. Utilizing online entertainment, customary news sources, and other correspondence channels can assist NGOs with countering deception and fabricate a positive public picture.

Mechanical Difficulties:

The fast progression of innovation brings the two open doors and difficulties for NGOs. While innovation can improve correspondence, support, and program execution, it likewise presents difficulties connected with advanced security, information assurance, and admittance to innovation in asset compelled conditions.

NGOs need to put resources into advanced education and network safety measures to safeguard delicate data and guarantee the protection of people engaged with their projects. Embracing mechanical progressions while staying aware of potential dangers is fundamental for remaining applicable in an undeniably computerized world.

Emergency Reaction and Crisis Readiness:

NGOs participated in philanthropic work face difficulties connected with emergency reaction and crisis readiness. Abrupt beginning fiascos, outfitted clashes, and general wellbeing crises require fast and all around composed reactions. Absence of readiness can prevent the viability of mediations notwithstanding dire and developing circumstances.

NGOs can address this test by creating extensive emergency reaction plans, directing customary penetrates, and laying out associations with different associations and neighborhood specialists. Building the ability to answer quickly to crises upgrades a NGO's capacity to meet the prompt necessities of impacted populaces.

Chapter 5

The Role of Media in Human Rights Advocacy

The job of media in common freedoms backing is critical, addressing a strong power that shapes public discernment, considers establishments responsible, and enhances the voices of the people who may somehow go unheard. In the cutting edge period, media, enveloping customary outlets, computerized stages, and resident news-casting, assumes a multi-layered part in propelling the reason for common liberties universally. This investigation digs into the complicated elements of the media's contribution in basic freedoms promotion, looking at its effect on mindfulness, responsibility, and the more extensive quest for equity.

Forming Public Discernment and Mindfulness:

Media fills in as a vital channel for molding public discernment and encouraging consciousness of basic freedoms issues. Through news inclusion, narratives, and insightful reporting, news sources carry basic freedoms infringement to the front of public cognizance. The visual and account force of media has the ability to bring out compassion, flash public talk, and brief aggregate activity.

News Announcing:

Conventional news sources, like papers, TV, and radio, assume a focal part in providing details regarding common freedoms infringement. Writers on the ground frequently act as observers to occasions, giving firsthand records that can impact general assessment. News announcing brings issues to light about issues going from political suppression and common freedoms to social treacheries, focusing on the situation of people and networks.

Narratives and Analytical News coverage:

Narratives and analytical news coverage offer top to bottom investigations of common liberties issues, giving a nuanced comprehension of the intricacies in question. Through convincing narrating, visual proof, and master investigation, these types of media shed light on foundational manhandles, reveal stowed away bits of insight, and challenge winning accounts. Narratives like "The Demonstration of Killing" and "For Sama" have been instrumental in uncovering common freedoms abominations.

Online Entertainment and Resident News coverage:

The coming of online entertainment has democratized the spread of data, empowering resident columnists and activists to assume an immediate part in basic liberties promotion. Stages like Twitter, Facebook, and Instagram act as moment courses for sharing stories, pictures, and recordings that may not get standard consideration. Developments, for example, #BlackLivesMatter and #MeToo have picked up speed through virtual entertainment, highlighting its effect in preparing popular assessment.

Considering Foundations Responsible:

Media fills in as a guard dog, holding legislatures, organizations, and strong elements responsible for their activities. Insightful news-casting, openness of debasement, and basic examination add to a culture of responsibility that is fundamental for the security and advancement of common freedoms.

Uncovering Debasement and Maltreatments of Force:

Analytical news-casting assumes a critical part in uncovering defilement and maltreatments of force, the two of which can prompt basic freedoms infringement. News sources direct inside and out examinations that uncover misbehaviors, carrying them to public consideration. The Panama Papers, for example, uncovered the degree of worldwide tax avoidance and monetary indecency, provoking boundless calls for responsibility.

Investigating Struggle and Monstrosities:

In locales tormented by struggle and outrages, media inclusion turns into a pivotal device for responsibility. Columnists and news associations revealing from struggle zones give imperative data about denials of basic freedoms, atrocities, and infringement of global helpful regulation. The covering the Rohingya emergency and the Syrian nationwide conflict features the job of media in uncovering the unforgiving real factors of contention.

Lawful Responsibility and Public Strain:

Media inclusion can catalyze lawful responsibility and public strain. Openness of denials of basic freedoms frequently prompts legitimate examinations and preliminaries, as well as global judgment. Prominent occasions incorporate the Global Lawbreaker Court's examinations concerning atrocities in Darfur and the tension applied on companies to resolve issues, for example, youngster work and ecological debasement.

Intensifying Underestimated Voices:

Media fills in as a stage to enhance the voices of minimized networks, guaranteeing that their accounts are heard and their battles recognized. By giving a space to these voices, media adds to a more comprehensive and delegate talk on basic freedoms.

Featuring Segregation and Bad form:

Media assumes a basic part in featuring separation and foul play looked by underestimated gatherings. Whether it is the LGBTQ+ people group, native people groups, or ethnic minorities, media inclusion uncovered foundational imbalances, biased practices, and basic liberties infringement. Such perceivability adds to backing endeavors for strategy changes and cultural acknowledgment.

Giving a Stage to Activists and Backers:

Common freedoms activists and promoters frequently depend on media stages to pass on their messages and draw in with a more extensive crowd. Interviews, commentaries, and component stories give a stage to activists to share their viewpoints, articulate the criticalness of their causes, and prepare public help. Media fills in as a scaffold between grassroots developments and the more extensive public.

Encouraging Social and Social Change:

Media can possibly encourage social and social change by testing imbued biases and advancing inclusivity. Portrayals in media impact cultural discernments, and positive depictions of minimized networks add to destroying generalizations. Media crusades that challenge biased rehearses, for example, the "No Disdain Discourse Development," plan to make a more open minded and fair society.

Challenges and Moral Contemplations:

While media assumes a vital part in common freedoms support, it isn't without its difficulties and moral contemplations.

Particular Revealing and Inclination:

Particular revealing and predisposition can shape accounts in manners that contort the truth of common liberties issues. Media associations might focus on specific stories over others, prompting uneven characters in inclusion. Furthermore, predisposition in detailing can sustain generalizations, building up existing biases and obstructing endeavors for true comprehension.

Drama and Injury Double-dealing:

Sentimentality, the accentuation on sensational or sincerely charged parts of a story, can think twice about respectability of detailing. The emphasis on realistic pictures and awful stories, while standing out, raises moral worries about the likely abuse of languishing over media utilization. Finding some kind of harmony between bringing issues to light and regarding the poise of those impacted is a fragile test.

Security Dangers for Columnists:

Writers giving an account of common freedoms issues frequently face critical security chances. In struggle zones and regions with harsh systems, writers might be exposed to dangers, brutality, or even designated assaults. The security of writers is a central concern, and media associations should focus on measures to safeguard their correspondents in testing conditions.

Business Tensions and Proprietorship Impact:

Business pressures and the impact of media proprietorship can influence the publication freedom of media sources. The quest for higher appraisals, promoting income, or arrangement with proprietorship interests might think twice about capacity of media associations to give fair-minded and objective inclusion of common liberties issues. This highlights the requirement for assorted and free media scenes.

Advanced Disinformation and Control:

The ascent of advanced media has delivered difficulties connected with disinformation and control. The spread of misleading data, deepfakes, and online control missions can subvert the believability of basic liberties revealing. Reality checking and media proficiency become fundamental apparatuses in fighting the disintegration of trust brought about by computerized deception.

The Developing Scene:

As innovation keeps on reshaping the media scene, new open doors and difficulties arise for common liberties promotion.

Advanced Activism and Worldwide Availability:

Computerized stages engage people to participate in activism and promotion on a worldwide scale. Hashtags, viral missions, and online petitions empower quick assembly and fortitude across borders. The Middle Easterner Spring and the #FeesMustFall development in South Africa are instances of computerized activism catalyzing social and political change.

Mechanical Advancements for Documentation:

Progressions in innovation, including cell phones and robots, empower more compelling documentation of denials of basic freedoms. Residents and activists can catch ongoing film, giving quick proof of infringement. This documentation turns into an incredible asset for backing, judicial procedures, and bringing issues to light.

Control and Web Closures:

Conversely, harsh state run administrations might fall back on restriction and web closures to smother dispute and control the story. This represents an immediate danger to computerized common freedoms support. Beating such difficulties requires a purposeful work to evade control, guarantee computerized security, and backing the option to get to data on the web.

5.1 Media's Influence on Public Opinion

The impact of media on popular assessment is an intricate and diverse peculiarity that fundamentally shapes the manner in which people see and figure out their general surroundings. Media, enveloping customary outlets, online stages, and web-based entertainment, fills in as an essential wellspring of data, an outlining specialist for occasions, and a pivotal go between in the development of cultural stories. This investigation dives into the systems through which media impacts popular assessment, looking at its job in plan setting, outlining, and molding aggregate mentalities toward different issues.

Plan Setting:

One of the principal manners by which media impacts popular assessment is through plan setting. This hypothesis places that media has the ability to feature explicit issues, occasions, or points, subsequently affecting the public's view of what is significant or important. The conspicuousness given to specific stories in the media plan can fundamentally affect the notability of those issues in the personalities of general society.

Media Choice and Prioritization:

The decisions made by news sources with respect to which stories to cover and how noticeably to include them add to plan setting.

First page titles, ideal time news inclusion, and moving subjects via online entertainment stages all assume a part in figuring out what catches the public's consideration. News sources go about as guardians, impacting the public plan by choosing, outlining, and focusing on reports.

Political Plan Setting:

In the domain of legislative issues, media assumes an essential part in forming the public's impression of policy centered issues and competitors. Political missions and strategy discusses frequently unfurl in the media scene, with inclusion affecting popular assessment on applicants' personality, strategy positions, and the meaning of specific issues. The media's emphasis on specific parts of political talk can influence public mentalities and needs.

Worldwide Plan Setting:

Media shapes public plans as well as impacts the worldwide story. Inclusion of worldwide occasions, clashes, and emergencies can affect popular assessment on international strategy, philanthropic mediations, and worldwide issues. The outlining of worldwide occasions by news sources adds to the arrangement of public mentalities toward various countries and areas.

Outlining:

Media impacts popular assessment through outlining, which includes the choice and show of data such that shapes the understanding of an issue. The outlining of reports impacts how crowds see the causes, results, and answers for different issues. Various casings can prompt dissimilar popular assessments on a similar issue.

Outline Choice and Tone:

News sources utilize explicit casings to introduce reports, accentuating specific parts of an issue while making light of others. Casings can be topical, zeroing in on the human effect, financial ramifications, or strategy aspects of a story. The tone and language utilized in news revealing likewise add to outlining, affecting the profound reaction and translation of occasions.

Political Outlining:

In the political circle, media outlining essentially impacts public view of political entertainers, gatherings, and philosophies. Political outlining shapes stories around strategy discussions, decisions, and government activities. Whether a strategy is outlined as "favorable to business" or "supportive of laborer" can significantly affect public help or resistance.

Social and Social Outlining:

Media assumes a part in outlining social and social issues, forming public mentalities toward subjects like race, orientation, and character. The outlining of social issues impacts public talk and can add to the arrangement of cultural standards and values. Media portrayal, or scarcity in that department, can sustain or challenge generalizations and predispositions.

The Job of Online Entertainment:

The approach of online entertainment has acquainted new elements with the connection among media and general assessment. Online entertainment stages act as the two enhancers of conventional media accounts and special spaces for client produced content, conversations, and developments.

Intensification of Conventional Media Accounts:

Web-based entertainment stages enhance customary media accounts by filling in as dispersion channels for reports. The sharing, retweeting, and remarking on news stories add to the dispersal of explicit points of view and edges. The viral idea of virtual entertainment can prompt the quick spread of specific stories, impacting a more extensive crowd.

Client Created Content and Resident Reporting:

Web-based entertainment empowers client created content, transforming normal people into supporters of the media scene. Resident newscasting, where people report on occasions and offer their points of view, has turned into a strong power. Online entertainment stages give a space to different voices and elective stories that may not track down articulation in conventional news sources.

Channel Air pockets and Protected, closed off areas:

Virtual entertainment calculations add to the formation of channel air pockets and closed quarters, where clients are presented to content that lines up with their current convictions and inclinations. This particular openness can support previous sentiments and limit openness to assorted viewpoints. The separate idea of online networks can add to enraptured popular sentiments.

Influence on Political Mentalities and Conduct:

Media's effect on popular assessment stretches out to political perspectives and conduct, molding people's perspectives on policy centered issues, competitors, and government activities.

Political Socialization:

Media assumes a significant part in the political socialization of people, forming how they might interpret municipal obligations, political belief systems, and government capabilities. News inclusion and political discourse add to the arrangement of political perspectives during basic phases of a singular's turn of events.

Political Trust and Doubt:

The manner in which media covers political occasions can impact levels of trust or doubt in political establishments. One-sided or sensationalized detailing might add to public distrust, while straightforward and objective reporting can cultivate trust. The connection between media depiction and public trust is proportional, with media reflecting and affecting public feeling.

Political Support and Casting a ballot Conduct:

Media impacts political support by illuminating residents about races, applicants, and strategy issues. Political missions decisively use media to speak with electors, and media inclusion can affect citizen impression of applicants. Media likewise shapes the public plan during races, affecting the issues that electors focus on.

Challenges and Moral Contemplations:

While media's impact on popular assessment is significant, it isn't without challenges and moral contemplations.

Journalistic spin and Objectivity:

Journalistic spin, whether saw or genuine, can affect the objectivity of information detailing. One-sided outlining and specific inclusion can add to slanted public discernments. Guaranteeing editorial uprightness, truth checking, and giving different points of view are fundamental to keeping up with media believability.

Melodrama and Misleading content:

The quest for crowd commitment and evaluations can prompt emotionalism and the utilization of misleading content, where titles are intended to snatch consideration instead of give precise data. This can add to falsehood and twist public comprehension of complicated issues.

Control and Disinformation:

The ascent of disinformation missions and media control represents a huge test. Bogus accounts, deepfakes, and deception can spread quickly, influencing general feelings and planting strife. Media education and strong truth checking components are fundamental for battling these difficulties.

5.2 Media Coverage Impacting Human Rights

Media inclusion assumes an essential part in forming public mindfulness, impacting strategy choices, and encouraging worldwide discussions on common freedoms issues. The capacity of news sources to enlighten treacheries, enhance underestimated voices, and consider culprits responsible is instrumental in propelling the reason for common freedoms.

This investigation digs into the complex effect of media inclusion on basic liberties, looking at how it shapes public insight, triggers global reactions, and explores moral contemplations.

Forming Public Discernment:

Media inclusion fills in as a powerful device for molding public impression of common liberties issues, outlining stories that can evoke compassion, prod activity, or support generalizations.

Adapting Accounts of Unfairness:

Through convincing narrating, media can refine the narratives of people confronting denials of basic freedoms, making these issues interesting to a worldwide crowd. Individual stories, whether passed on through composed articles, narratives, or visual narrating, have the ability to inspire compassion and encourage a feeling of shared humankind. This adaptation is especially significant in accumulating public help for civil rights aims.

Outlining Denials of basic liberties:

The outlining of denials of basic liberties in media inclusion essentially impacts public comprehension. The decision of language, pictures, and stories can shape view of casualties, culprits, and the more extensive setting of infringement. News sources have the obligation to approach stories in a manner that precisely mirrors the intricacies of basic liberties issues and tries not to propagate generalizations or predispositions.

Bringing issues to light of Underreported Issues:

Media inclusion can reveal insight into underreported basic liberties issues, carrying them to the front of public cognizance. Issues that might be minimized or ignored are given perceivability through insightful news coverage, narratives, and missions. This expanded mindfulness is vital for assembling public help and making tension for fundamental change.

Worldwide Reactions and Support:

Media inclusion fills in as an impetus for global reactions, impacting political activities, preparing grassroots developments, and giving a stage to support.

Political Tension and Responsibility:

High-profile media inclusion can apply political tension on state run administrations and substances associated with denials of basic freedoms. Openness in the worldwide media spotlight might provoke judgment from different countries, calls for examinations, and authorizations. The danger of reputational harm, enhanced by media inclusion, can go about as an impetus for responsibility and restorative activities.

Preparing Grassroots Developments:

Media inclusion has the ability to prepare grassroots developments and common society associations. At the point when denials of basic liberties are uncovered, concerned residents and activists can use media accounts to bring issues to light, arrange fights, and supporter for strategy changes. Virtual entertainment stages further intensify these endeavors, working with the fast assembly of worldwide fortitude missions.

Molding Worldwide Insights:

The depiction of basic freedoms issues in the media impacts how countries and networks are seen on the worldwide stage. Nations might try to deal with their worldwide picture because of media inclusion, perceiving the likely effect on strategic relations, economic accords, and global organizations. Media accounts add to molding the worldwide local area's position on basic liberties rehearses.

Moral Contemplations and Difficulties:

While media inclusion assumes a critical part in common liberties promotion, it likewise wrestles with moral contemplations and difficulties that request cautious route.

Adjusting Awareness and Honesty:

The media faces the test of adjusting aversion to casualties of denials of basic liberties with the basic of honesty. Realistic pictures, horrendous accounts, and express subtleties might convey the gravity of infringement yet can likewise risk retraumatizing people and sensationalizing languishing. Editorial morals request cautious thought of the likely effect on casualties and crowds.

Staying away from Generalizations and Inclination:

Media inclusion should try not to propagate generalizations and inclinations that can add to misperceptions of people or networks impacted by denials of basic freedoms. The outlining of stories, the choice of sources, and the language utilized ought to be directed by a promise to reasonableness, precision, and social responsiveness. Writers should be watchful against unexpected predispositions that might saturate their detailing.

Safeguarding Weak Populaces:

Covering basic liberties issues including weak populaces, like exiles, youngsters, or casualties of sexual savagery, requires extraordinary consideration. News sources should focus on the assurance of people in danger and comply with moral rules that shield their protection and pride. Assent, obscurity, and informed announcing are significant contemplations in covering such touchy issues.

Staying away from Instrumentalization:

Common liberties issues ought not be instrumentalized for political plans or drama. Media inclusion should focus on the quest for truth, free news-casting, and the moral obligation to illuminate the general population. Keeping away from the control of human languishing over philosophical designs is fundamental for keeping up with the respectability of revealing.

Media's Part in Responsibility News-casting:

Media assumes an imperative part in considering culprits responsible for denials of basic liberties through insightful reporting and openness of fundamental treacheries.

Analytical Announcing:

Insightful news coverage fills in as a foundation of responsibility, revealing secret maltreatments, defilement, and fundamental disappointments. Top to bottom examinations by news sources can uncover the main drivers of common liberties infringement, uncover examples of wrongdoing, and hold establishments, legislatures, or partnerships responsible.

Informant Insurance:

Media inclusion frequently depends on data given by informants who risk their security to uncover bad behavior. Safeguarding informants is a basic moral thought, as they assume an essential part in bringing denials of basic freedoms to the public's consideration. Lawful structures and editorial practices should focus on the wellbeing and obscurity of the people who approach.

Cultivating Straightforwardness and Public Investigation:

Media inclusion cultivates straightforwardness by exposing people with great influence to public examination. Denials of basic freedoms flourish in conditions of mystery and unrestrained power. Insightful detailing and openness add to a culture of straightforwardness, empowering general society to consider specialists responsible and request equity.

Challenges in Mindful Detailing:

Media faces difficulties in capably writing about common liberties issues, especially in areas with prohibitive administration structures and elevated security gambles.

Oversight and Constraint:

News sources working in locales with tyrant systems might confront oversight, suppression, and lawful dangers. Columnists giving an account of denials of basic freedoms in these conditions face the test of exploring limitations while maintaining moral principles. Joint efforts with global media associations and support bunches become fundamental for security.

Security Dangers for Columnists:

Investigating denials of basic freedoms frequently opens writers to security gambles, including dangers, viciousness, and provocation. Media associations should focus on the security of their correspondents, giving preparation, assets, and backing. Worldwide fortitude and support can assume an essential part in requesting the security of columnists working in hazardous conditions.

Exploring Social Awarenesses:

Providing details regarding basic freedoms issues in socially different settings requires a nuanced comprehension of neighborhood responsive qualities. Slips up in social portrayal can prompt errors and ruin the viability of media accounts. News sources should put resources into social skill, draw in nearby points of view, and focus on joint effort with columnists from impacted networks.

5.3 Media's Responsibility in Promoting Human Rights

The job of media in advancing common liberties is necessary to the working of vote based social orders, filling in as a urgent extension between people with great influence and general society. News sources bear the obligation of maintaining moral principles, encouraging straightforwardness, and pushing for civil rights. This investigation dives into the complex obligations of the media in advancing basic freedoms, looking at its part in responsibility, mindfulness, and the development of an educated and connected with populace.

Cultivating Responsibility and Straightforwardness:

Insightful News-casting as an Impetus for Responsibility:

Insightful reporting assumes a focal part in holding people, foundations, and legislatures responsible for denials of basic liberties. News sources are answerable for revealing secret bits of insight, uncovering defilement, and revealing insight into foundational shameful acts. Through inside and out examinations, writers act as guard dogs, inciting remedial activities and adding to the foundation of a culture of responsibility.

Informant Insurance and the Right to Data:

Media's liability stretches out to safeguarding informants who assume a vital part in exposing denials of basic liberties. Giving a stage to people to uncover unfortunate behavior or bad behavior is fundamental for straightforwardness. News sources should explore legitimate structures to guarantee the wellbeing and secrecy of informants, perceiving their indispensable commitment to responsibility reporting.

Upholding for the Right to Data:

Media has an obligation to advocate for and safeguard the right to data as a principal basic freedom. By requesting admittance to government reports, encouraging a culture of straightforwardness, and testing prohibitive regulations, news sources add to the public's capacity to consider foundations responsible. The right to data is a foundation in the battle against debasement and denials of basic liberties.

Bringing issues to light and Catalyzing Activity:

Adapting Stories to Summon Compassion:

Media's liability in advancing basic freedoms incorporates acculturating stories to bring out compassion and encourage understanding. Through convincing accounts, visual narrating, and effective revealing, news sources have the ability to bring the appearances and accounts of those impacted by denials of basic liberties to the front. This acculturation is essential in preparing public help and catalyzing activity.

Revealing Insight into Underreported Issues:

Media has an obligation to reveal insight into underreported common freedoms issues, guaranteeing that minimized voices and dismissed emergencies get consideration. By focusing on inclusion of less noticeable issues, news sources add to a more extensive comprehension of the worldwide common freedoms scene. This mindfulness is fundamental for creating public talk and provoking global reactions.

Teaching The general population on Freedoms as well as limitations:

News sources assume a part in teaching people in general about basic liberties standards, regulations, and obligations. Through news highlights, narratives, and assessment pieces, media adds to the dispersal of data that enables people to grasp their freedoms as well as certain limitations in a popularity based society. Informed residents are better prepared to take part in backing and request responsibility.

Advocating Variety, Inclusivity, and Non-Separation:

Trying not to Generalizations and Advance Comprehensive Portrayal:

Media has an obligation to try not to sustain generalizations and predispositions that add to separation. By advancing comprehensive portrayal and various points of view, news sources add to destroying hurtful generalizations and encouraging a more comprehensive and open minded society. Dependable detailing requires a promise to fair and precise portrayal across different social, social, and character aspects.

Intensifying Minimized Voices:

News sources are entrusted with intensifying the voices of minimized networks and people. Raising the viewpoints of those frequently avoided or underrepresented in standard talk is fundamental for tending to foundational imbalances. Media's obligation to giving a stage to different voices adds to civil rights and difficulties biased rehearses.

Advocating LGBTQ+ Privileges and Orientation Uniformity:

Media's liability stretches out to advocating LGBTQ+ privileges and advancing orientation equity. By testing generalizations, giving perceivability to LGBTQ+ people group, and resolving issues connected with orientation based viciousness and segregation, news sources add to cultivating a more comprehensive and impartial society. Mindful revealing includes testing cultural standards that sustain segregation in light of sexual direction or orientation.

Exploring Moral Contemplations:

Adjusting Awareness and Honesty:

News sources should explore the fragile harmony between aversion to casualties of denials of basic liberties and the basic of honesty. Moral revealing includes cautious thought of the likely effect of realistic pictures or express subtleties on casualties and crowds. Finding some kind of harmony guarantees mindful detailing that regards the pride of those impacted.

Keeping away from Emotionalism and Double-dealing:

Mindful detailing requires news sources to keep away from drama and the double-dealing of human languishing over the purpose of viewership or readership. Maintaining editorial morals implies focusing on the quest for truth over hair-raising accounts and regarding the security and prosperity of those straightforwardly affected by denials of basic freedoms.

Basic Commitment with Sources and Data:

Media's liability in advancing common liberties includes fundamentally captivating with sources and data. Confirming the exactness of data, reality checking, and cross-referring to are fundamental practices to guarantee the unwavering quality of revealing. In a period of deception, news sources assume a basic part in maintaining the trustworthiness of data imparted to people in general.

Difficulties and Responsibility in the Time of Advanced Media:

Combatting Disinformation and Falsehood:

In the time of computerized media, battling disinformation and deception is a critical test. News sources should go to proactive lengths to reality actually look at data before spread, advance media education, and counter bogus accounts that can sabotage public comprehension of common liberties issues.

Exploring Online Entertainment Stages:

Media's liability stretches out to exploring the effect of virtual entertainment stages on the scattering of data. While these stages give valuable open doors to boundless conveyance, they additionally present difficulties connected with the fast spread of falsehood, closed quarters, and algorithmic predispositions. Dependable revealing includes understanding and alleviating these difficulties.

Guaranteeing Publication Freedom:

News sources should guarantee publication freedom to maintain their obligation in advancing basic liberties. Difficulties like corporate interests, political tensions, and promoter impact can think twice about freedom of newsrooms. Defending article independence is fundamental for keeping up with the trustworthiness and validity of detailing.

Chapter 6

Economic, Social, and Cultural Rights

The domain of basic freedoms stretches out past the political and common aspects to envelop Monetary, Social, and Social Privileges (ESCR). Established in the comprehension that nobility and opportunity are personally attached to financial prosperity, ESCR structure a vital piece of the more extensive common liberties system. This investigation dives into the complicated embroidery of Financial, Social, and Social Freedoms, looking at their importance, challenges in execution, and the interconnected idea of these privileges in encouraging a fair and evenhanded society.

Characterizing Monetary, Social, and Social Freedoms:

Monetary, Social, and Social Freedoms, as expressed in different peaceful accords, envelop a scope of privileges that are central to human nobility and prosperity. These freedoms incorporate the option to work, the right to schooling, the right to wellbeing, the right to a sufficient way of life, the right to social support, and the option to partake in the advantages of logical advancement, among others.

Not at all like common and political privileges, which center around individual opportunities and political interest, ESCR stress the aggregate and cultural aspects fundamental for the full acknowledgment of human potential.

The Option to Work:

The option to work embodies the thought that each individual has the privilege to pick and partake in beneficial business uninhibitedly. It incorporates the right to simply and positive states of work, the option to approach valuable open doors, and the option to frame and join worker's organizations. This right recognizes the inherent connection between one's work and their financial and social standing.

The Right to Instruction:

The right to schooling perceives that everybody has the option to access and profit from a comprehensive, quality instruction. This includes essential schooling, optional instruction, advanced education, and professional preparation. Training isn't just a method for self-improvement yet additionally a urgent calculate tending to cultural disparities and cultivating educated and drew in residents.

The Right to Wellbeing:

The right to wellbeing attests that everybody has the option to partake in the most elevated achievable norm of physical and psychological well-being. This incorporates admittance to medical care administrations, disinfection, and fundamental prescriptions. Wellbeing isn't just a singular concern however a cultural resource, and the acknowledgment of this right adds to the general prosperity of networks.

The Right to a Satisfactory Way of life:

This right perceives that everybody has the privilege to a satisfactory way of life for them as well as their families, including food, dress, lodging, and essential social administrations. It highlights the significance of tending to destitution and guaranteeing that people can live in pride and security.

The Right to Social Interest:

Social privileges recognize the significance of protecting and encouraging social variety. This incorporates the option to partake in social life, partake in the advantages of logical advancement, and advantage from one's own commitments to social undertakings. Social privileges accentuate the characteristic worth of different social articulations and their part in advancing society.

Interconnected Nature of Monetary, Social, and Social Freedoms:

The interconnectedness of Monetary, Social, and Social Freedoms is an essential part of their acknowledgment. These freedoms are not disengaged classifications but instead structure a coordinated system, each building up and supporting the others. The failure to appreciate one right might obstruct the acknowledgment of others, making a perplexing web where financial imbalance can influence admittance to schooling, and absence of admittance to medical services can thwart the option to work.

The Effect of Schooling on Financial Open doors:

The right to schooling is an impetus for financial strengthening. Admittance to quality schooling furnishes people with the abilities and information important to partake in the labor force, consequently improving their financial open doors. A knowledgeable populace adds to monetary turn of events, development, and social advancement.

Wellbeing as an Essential for Financial Cooperation:

The right to wellbeing is fundamental for financial efficiency. A solid populace is bound to connect effectively in the labor force, adding to financial development. On the other hand, deficient admittance to medical services can bring about a less useful labor force, blocking a country's financial potential.

The Job of Sufficient Way of life in Guaranteeing Pride:

The right to a sufficient way of life is essential to guaranteeing human respect. Destitution and hardship influence a singular's material prosperity as well as effect their capacity to take part in friendly and social life completely. Monetary security is an essential for the satisfaction in different privileges.

Social Interest and Social Consideration:

Social freedoms, including the right to social support, add to social attachment and consideration. Social articulation encourages a feeling of personality and having a place, which, thusly, can decidedly influence emotional wellness and prosperity. At the point when people are allowed to partake in social life, it improves the general structure holding the system together.

Aggregate Advantages of Logical Advancement:

The option to partake in the advantages of logical advancement features the aggregate idea of progressions. Logical advancement not just adds to individual prosperity through clinical leap forwards yet in addition has more extensive cultural ramifications, impacting financial turn of events, ecological maintainability, and generally friendly advancement.

Challenges in the Execution of Monetary, Social, and Social Freedoms:

While the acknowledgment of Monetary, Social, and Social Freedoms is revered in peaceful accords and public constitutions, the execution of these privileges faces various difficulties, going from asset limitations to primary imbalances and deficient legitimate systems.

Asset Imperatives and Prioritization:

One of the essential difficulties in executing ESCR is the impediment of assets. States and foundations might confront contending requests for restricted assets, making it trying to focus on monetary, social, and social freedoms. Asset imperatives can bring about deficient interests in training, medical care, and social administrations.

Underlying Disparities and Separation:

Underlying imbalances, including orientation based separation, racial differences, and financial partitions, present huge obstructions to the full acknowledgment of ESCR. Oppressive practices can bring about inconsistent admittance to schooling, work, and medical care, sustaining patterns of destitution and rejection.

Absence of Legitimate Acknowledgment and Enforceability:

In certain wards, Financial, Social, and Social Freedoms might need unequivocal lawful acknowledgment and enforceability. Dissimilar to common and political freedoms, the justiciability of ESCR can be restricted, making it provoking for people to look for lawful cures in instances of infringement. This subverts the viability of these freedoms practically speaking.

Worldwide Financial Imbalances:

Financial globalization has prompted expanded interconnectedness however has additionally exacerbated worldwide monetary disparities. The advantages of financial advancement are not similarly dispersed, with underestimated networks and agricultural countries frequently enduring the worst part of monetary variations. Tending to these worldwide imbalances is significant for the exhaustive acknowledgment of ESCR.

The Job of Global Participation and Fortitude:

Given the worldwide idea of monetary, social, and social difficulties, global participation and fortitude assume a urgent part in propelling the acknowledgment of ESCR. Cooperative endeavors among countries, worldwide associations, and common society are fundamental for tending to cross-line issues, for example, neediness, environmental change, and wellbeing emergencies.

Worldwide Basic liberties Instruments:

Worldwide basic liberties instruments, like the Global Contract on Monetary, Social, and Social Freedoms (ICESCR), give a system to aggregate activity. Approving countries focus on doing whatever it may take to dynamically understand these privileges, both exclusively and through global participation.

Improvement Help and Help:

Improvement help and help programs add to cultivating monetary and social advancement in distraught locales. By offering monetary and specialized help, more prosperous countries can assist with tending to the asset imperatives looked by emerging nations, advancing the satisfaction of ESCR.

Environment Equity and Ecological Manageability:

Environmental change, with its significant effect on occupations, wellbeing, and social scenes, is an issue that requires worldwide collaboration. Environment equity underscores the need to address the lopsided effect of natural debasement on weak networks, perceiving the interconnectedness of ecological privileges with monetary and social freedoms.

6.1 Economic Disparities and Human Rights

The unavoidable issue of monetary inconsistencies creates a long shaded area over the scene of basic liberties, uncovering perplexing associations between financial imbalances and the more extensive system of human nobility. This investigation digs into the perplexing interaction between financial differences and common freedoms, inspecting the broad outcomes of imbalance on admittance to major privileges, open doors, and generally prosperity.

The Effect of Monetary Differences on Basic freedoms:

Right to a Satisfactory Way of life:

Monetary differences straightforwardly influence the acknowledgment of the right to a sufficient way of life. The capacity to get to fundamental necessities like food, lodging, and medical services is dependent upon one's monetary standing. In social orders set apart by immense pay holes, minimized populaces frequently wind up prohibited from the advantages of financial advancement, undermining their capacity to carry on with an existence of nobility.

Right to Training:

Monetary disparities fundamentally influence the right to schooling. Wealthy people approach quality instruction, including non-public schools and extra instructive assets, while monetarily hindered networks frequently wrestle with underfunded state funded schools and restricted open doors for advanced education. This difference sustains patterns of destitution and impedes social versatility.

Right to Work:

The option to work is unpredictably connected to financial variations. Inconsistent circulation of open positions, wage holes, and unfair business practices can restrict admittance to good work for minimized gatherings. Monetary imbalances manifest in variations in employer stability, fair wages, and open doors for proficient headway.

Right to Wellbeing:

Monetary variations add to abberations in wellbeing results, affecting the right to wellbeing. Admittance to quality medical services administrations, preventive measures, and clinical therapies is in many cases slanted for those with higher financial status. Financial variables, including lodging conditions and admittance to nutritious food, assume a significant part in deciding wellbeing results.

Right to Government managed retirement:

Monetary variations sabotage the right to federal retirement aide. Weak populaces confronting monetary difficulty frequently need satisfactory social assurance instruments. Lacking government managed retirement measures compound the effect of financial shocks, leaving minimized people without a wellbeing net to safeguard them from neediness and hardship.

Underlying Disparities and Separation:

Orientation Imbalance and Financial Incongruities:

Orientation based financial incongruities sustain fundamental disparities. By and large, procure not exactly their male partners, face restricted admittance to financial assets, and experience obstructions to monetary strengthening. Orientation based separation in the working environment further adds to financial differences, restricting ladies' capacity to completely practice their privileges.

Racial and Ethnic Differences:

Financial imbalances are frequently entwined with racial and ethnic abberations. Verifiable treacheries, prejudicial practices, and foundational inclinations add to inconsistent financial open doors for racial and ethnic minorities. From work valuable chances to admittance to quality training, these inconsistencies highlight the interconnection of financial and social disparities.

Native Freedoms and Monetary Underestimation:

Native people group overall wrestle with financial underestimation, frequently connected to authentic dispossession and double-dealing. Restricted admittance to assets, prejudicial strategies, and an absence of financial open doors sustain destitution inside native populaces, impinging upon their capacity to partake in a scope of basic liberties.

Inability and Monetary Disparities:

People with handicaps face monetary abberations because of hindrances in schooling, business, and openness. Unfair practices limit their admittance to the gig market, prompting higher paces of joblessness and monetary reliance. Tending to financial abberations for people with handicaps requires destroying obstructions to full support in the public arena.

Challenges in Tending to Monetary Differences:

Worldwide Financial Imbalances:

The worldwide financial scene is set apart by unmistakable disparities among wealthy and emerging countries. Primary issues, including out of line exchange rehearses, obligation weights, and restricted admittance to assets, add to the propagation of monetary incongruities on a worldwide scale. Tending to these difficulties requires worldwide collaboration and a guarantee to evenhanded financial strategies.

Political Will and Strategy Measures:

Handling monetary differences requires political will and exhaustive approach measures. States assume a critical part in carrying out moderate tax collection, social government assistance projects, and measures that guarantee impartial dissemination of assets. Lacking political will or approaches that favor financial elites can propagate inconsistencies and prevent the acknowledgment of basic liberties for all.

Admittance to Equity and Legitimate Securities:

Financial differences frequently convert into variations in admittance to equity. Underestimated people group, confronting financial difficulty, may experience hindrances to legitimate portrayal and security. Reinforcing lawful structures that address financial shameful acts, advance work freedoms, and battle oppressive practices is pivotal for tending to variations at the foundational level.

Monetary Variations With regards to One side to Advancement:

Right to Advancement and Comprehensive Development:

The right to advancement underscores the requirement for fair, comprehensive, and feasible turn of events.

Financial inconsistencies obstruct the acknowledgment of this right by propagating prohibition and restricting the advantages of improvement to specific portions of the populace. Comprehensive development that tends to monetary abberations is fundamental for encouraging certified and enduring turn of events.

Supportable Advancement Objectives (SDGs):

The Reasonable Advancement Objectives perceive the interconnected idea of monetary, social, and natural difficulties. Objective 10, explicitly, accentuates the need to decrease imbalances inside and among nations. Accomplishing the SDGs requires designated endeavors to address monetary variations and guarantee that the advantages of improvement are shared by all.

Job of Common Society and Promotion:

Common Society's Guard dog Job:

Common society associations assume an essential part as guard dogs, upholding for the freedoms of underestimated networks and considering states and organizations responsible for monetary treacheries. Through research, mindfulness crusades, and grassroots preparation, common society adds to molding approaches that address monetary variations and safeguard basic liberties.

Enabling Underestimated People group:

Enabling underestimated networks is fundamental to tending to monetary incongruities. Drives that emphasis on schooling, professional preparation, and monetary strengthening programs add to breaking the patterns of destitution and encouraging independence. By intensifying the voices of those most impacted, common society can drive significant change.

6.2 Social and Cultural Challenges

Social and social provokes present complicated deterrents to the acknowledgment of common liberties, as they are profoundly interwoven with cultural standards, convictions, and authentic inheritances. This investigation dives into the multi-layered nature of social and social difficulties, looking at their effect on different common freedoms aspects, the perseverance of segregation, and the intricacies associated with cultivating social responsiveness and inclusivity.

The Impact of Social and Social Standards on Basic freedoms:

Orientation Imbalance:

Social and social standards frequently propagate orientation imbalance, affecting the acknowledgment of ladies' freedoms.

Oppressive practices, conventional orientation jobs, and generalizations add to inconsistent power elements, restricting ladies' admittance to schooling, work valuable open doors, and cooperation in dynamic cycles. Testing profoundly instilled orientation standards is critical for accomplishing orientation fairness and maintaining common freedoms for all.

Segregation In light of Sexual Direction and Orientation Personality:

Social and social difficulties manifest in victimization people in light of their sexual direction and orientation personality. Homophobia, transphobia, and cultural disgrace make hindrances to the happiness regarding major privileges for the LGBTQ+ people group. Encouraging a comprehensive culture that embraces variety is fundamental for destroying oppressive standards and guaranteeing equivalent freedoms for all.

Social Works on Affecting Wellbeing and Prosperity:

Social practices can impact wellbeing results and admittance to medical services. Unsafe conventional practices, like female genital mutilation or kid marriage, present huge difficulties to one side to wellbeing and real independence. Tending to these difficulties requires a sensitive harmony between regarding social variety and shielding the standards of basic liberties.

The Tirelessness of Segregation:

Racial and Ethnic Segregation:

Social and social difficulties frequently manifest in racial and ethnic segregation, influencing minimized networks around the world. Bias, generalizations, and foundational predispositions can bring about inconsistent open doors, racial profiling, and boundaries to approach cooperation in friendly, monetary, and political circles. Combatting prejudice requires tending to well established social perspectives and advancing inclusivity.

Strict Bigotry:

Social and strict standards can add to strict bigotry, influencing the opportunity of religion and conviction. Victimization strict minorities, limitations on strict practices, and cultural biases can reduce the privileges of people to communicate their convictions openly. Cultivating a culture of resistance and regard for different strict points of view is fundamental for safeguarding this key right.

Social Responsiveness and Inclusivity:

Offsetting Social Responsiveness with Basic liberties:

Exploring the convergence of social responsiveness and basic freedoms requires a nuanced approach.

While regarding social variety is essential, it ought not be utilized as a safeguard to legitimize rehearses that encroach upon crucial privileges. Finding some kind of harmony includes advancing social comprehension while immovably maintaining the general standards of basic liberties.

Advancing Inclusivity without Social Government:

Advancing inclusivity ought to be drawn nearer with watchfulness to stay away from social colonialism. Empowering different points of view and voices inside social orders is fundamental, however it ought not be finished to the detriment of minimizing or smothering specific social personalities. Perceiving the organization of networks to reclassify social standards, particularly those that abuse common freedoms, is essential.

Schooling as an Impetus for Social Change:

Schooling assumes a vital part in testing prejudicial social standards and encouraging social change. By consolidating comprehensive educational programs that celebrate variety, challenge generalizations, and advance decisive reasoning, social orders can add to destroying biased convictions and building a more comprehensive social ethos.

Challenges in Tending to Social and Social Difficulties:

Protection from Change:

Protection from change is a critical test in addressing social and social boundaries to common liberties. Profoundly instilled convictions and practices might confront obstruction from people, networks, or even state run administrations. Beating this obstruction requires complete mindfulness crusades, grassroots preparation, and support for social movements.

Lawful and Strategy Structures:

Creating lawful and strategy systems that figure out some kind of harmony between social awareness and common liberties security is testing. A few social practices might appreciate legitimate security, making it challenging to mediate in situations where common liberties infringement happen. Creating systems that regard social variety while shielding essential freedoms requires cautious thought and discourse.

Worldwide Viewpoints on Social Difficulties:

Universalism versus Relativism Discussion:

The pressure among universalism and social relativism shapes global points of view on tending to social difficulties. The universalist methodology affirms that specific common liberties are pertinent to all people paying little mind to social setting, while social relativism contends that freedoms ought to be figured out inside the social system of every general public.

Finding some kind of harmony that recognizes social variety while maintaining essential privileges stays an intricate global undertaking.

Global Common liberties Instruments:

Global common liberties components, for example, the Unified Countries Basic freedoms Board and deal bodies, assume a urgent part in tending to social difficulties. These discussions give spaces to exchange, examination, and suggestions to address common liberties infringement established in social practices. Drawing in with these systems considers a worldwide viewpoint on basic freedoms issues formed by social elements.

6.3 Global Efforts to Address Economic and Social Injustices

In a world set apart by stunning monetary differences and steady friendly treacheries, worldwide endeavors to resolve these issues have become vital for encouraging a more evenhanded and comprehensive worldwide society. This investigation dives into the multi-layered drives, procedures, and difficulties that describe worldwide undertakings to handle monetary and social treacheries, underscoring the significance of aggregate activity and global collaboration.

Worldwide Systems and Arrangements:

Maintainable Improvement Objectives (SDGs):

The Unified Countries' Maintainable Improvement Objectives (SDGs) stand as a complete outline for tending to financial and social treacheries worldwide. Incorporating 17 objectives, the SDGs plan to annihilate neediness, guarantee comprehensive and quality schooling, advance orientation balance, and decrease disparities. By giving a common structure, the SDGs urge countries to work all in all to accomplish normal targets, recognizing the interconnectedness of social and monetary difficulties.

Worldwide Work Association (ILO):

The Global Work Association assumes a vital part in advancing civil rights and fair work rehearses around the world. Through shows, suggestions, and specialized help, the ILO resolves issues, for example, kid work, constrained work, and separation in the work environment. Its endeavors add to molding a worldwide climate where financial open doors are all the more legitimately circulated, and laborers' privileges are shielded.

Advancing Fair Exchange and Financial Equity:

Fair Exchange Developments:

Fair exchange drives have picked up speed as a grassroots reaction to monetary treacheries in worldwide exchange.

Fair exchange standards focus on impartial wages, safe working circumstances, and ecological manageability. Affirmations and names assist purchasers with pursuing moral decisions, supporting items that stick to fair exchange principles. By advancing fair exchange rehearses, these developments add to making an all the more and empathetic worldwide financial framework.

Corporate Social Obligation (CSR):

Perceiving the persuasive job of enterprises in forming worldwide economies, the idea of Corporate Social Obligation has acquired noticeable quality. Organizations are progressively expected to go past benefit making and effectively add to social and ecological prosperity. CSR drives envelop moral strategic policies, local area commitment, and manageable improvement projects, cultivating a feeling of obligation and responsibility in the corporate area.

Worldwide Monetary Establishments and Financial Change:

World Bank and Global Financial Asset (IMF):

Worldwide monetary establishments, like the World Bank and the IMF, assume a huge part in molding worldwide financial strategies. These foundations give monetary help, strategy guidance, and specialized help to countries, especially those confronting financial difficulties. Nonetheless, reactions have been raised with respect to the conditionalities appended to advances, which some of the time worsen social disparities. Calls for change inside these foundations try to guarantee that their arrangements focus on civil rights and comprehensive turn of events.

Obligation Alleviation Drives:

Obligation help drives intend to ease the monetary weights of agricultural countries, permitting them to divert assets toward social projects and destitution decrease. The Vigorously Obliged Unfortunate Nations (HIPC) Drive and the Multilateral Obligation Help Drive (MDRI) embody worldwide endeavors to address the monetary treacheries originating from unreasonable obligation troubles. These drives recognize the requirement for a more evenhanded dispersion of worldwide assets.

Worldwide Wellbeing and Social Government assistance:

Worldwide Wellbeing Organizations:

Cooperative endeavors in worldwide wellbeing organizations address differences in medical services access and results. Drives like GAVI (the Immunization Union) and the Worldwide Asset to Battle Helps, Tuberculosis, and Intestinal sickness prepare assets and skill to handle wellbeing imbalances on a worldwide scale. These organizations feature the interconnectedness of wellbeing with more extensive financial issues and highlight the significance of aggregate activity.

Worldwide Guide and Advancement Help:

Unfamiliar guide and advancement help programs add to addressing social treacheries by offering monetary help to nations confronting financial difficulties. The worldwide local area perceives the ethical basic of helping countries out of luck and accomplishing practical turn of events.

Be that as it may, worries about help viability, conditionalities, and the requirement for a more evenhanded circulation of assets continue.

Challenges in Worldwide Endeavors:

Power Irregular characteristics and Worldwide Administration:

Relentless power irregular characteristics in worldwide administration structures present an impressive test to aggregate endeavors. The impact of strong countries and global organizations can shape strategies and upset the execution of drives that focus on financial and civil rights. Tending to these lopsided characteristics requires changes in worldwide administration designs to guarantee more impartial portrayal and navigation.

Political Will and Responsibility:

The outcome of worldwide endeavors to address financial and social shameful acts depends on the political will of countries and pioneers. In certain occasions, international contemplations, public interests, and contending needs can hinder the responsibility required for far reaching and supported activity. Building political will requires backing, public mindfulness, and conciliatory endeavors to focus on civil rights on the worldwide plan.

Environment Equity and Natural Treacheries:

The interweaved idea of natural issues with financial and social shameful acts adds intricacy to worldwide endeavors. Environmental change lopsidedly influences weak networks, fueling existing imbalances. Tending to environment equity includes perceiving authentic obligations, supporting transformation gauges, and guaranteeing that natural arrangements focus on the prosperity of minimized populaces.

Common Society and Grassroots Developments:

Common Society Support:

Common society associations assume a vital part in considering legislatures and foundations responsible for tending to monetary and social treacheries. Through support, mindfulness crusades, and grassroots preparation, common society goes about as an impetus for change. Their endeavors enhance the voices of minimized networks and add to forming worldwide accounts on civil rights.

Individuals Driven Developments:

Grassroots developments, driven by individuals straightforwardly impacted by financial and social treacheries, have become strong problem solvers. Developments like the People of color Matter development, worldwide youth environment strikes, and civil rights crusades outfit the aggregate force of networks to request foundational change. These developments underline the significance of inclusivity, multifacetedness, and individuals driven approaches in tending to worldwide difficulties.

Chapter 7

Emerging Technologies and Human Rights

The fast development of innovation in the 21st century has introduced exceptional progressions, changing the manner in which we live, work, and connect. Notwithstanding, as arising advances keep on reshaping our reality, they additionally bring up basic issues about their effect on common liberties. This investigation digs into the complicated exchange between arising advances and basic freedoms, looking at both the expected advantages and the moral difficulties that emerge in this consistently developing scene.

The Commitment of Arising Advances:

Man-made reasoning (computer based intelligence):

Man-made reasoning holds enormous commitment across different areas, from medical services and schooling to fund and transportation. Simulated intelligence calculations can improve effectiveness, robotize assignments, and dissect immense datasets, prompting creative answers for cultural difficulties.

In medical services, for instance, man-made intelligence can aid diagnostics, drug disclosure, and customized therapy plans, possibly further developing worldwide wellbeing results.

Web of Things (IoT):

The Web of Things, with its organization of interconnected gadgets, can possibly reform how we cooperate with our environmental factors. Shrewd urban areas, for example, influence IoT to upgrade metropolitan preparation, enhance asset portion, and work on the personal satisfaction for inhabitants. IoT likewise assumes a critical part in ecological checking, horticulture, and calamity the executives.

Blockchain Innovation:

Blockchain innovation, known for its decentralized and secure nature, has disturbed conventional frameworks, especially in finance. Digital forms of money, controlled by blockchain, offer monetary incorporation and empower cross-line exchanges. Past money, blockchain has applications in production network straightforwardness, character check, and guaranteeing the uprightness of computerized data.

Biotechnology and Genomics:

Progresses in biotechnology and genomics have opened new boondocks in medical services, agribusiness, and ecological preservation. Accuracy medication, empowered by genomics, tailors clinical medicines to individual hereditary profiles. In horticulture, hereditary designing can upgrade crop versatility and decrease natural effect, adding to worldwide food security.

Common liberties Suggestions:

Security Concerns:

The unavoidable assortment and investigation of individual information, driven by artificial intelligence and IoT, raise huge protection concerns. Reconnaissance advances, facial acknowledgment frameworks, and information profiling can encroach upon the right to protection. Finding some kind of harmony between mechanical development and defending individual security is a basic test in the computerized age.

Algorithmic Inclination and Segregation:

Simulated intelligence frameworks, depending on immense datasets, can acquire and sustain predispositions present in those datasets. Algorithmic predisposition can bring about biased results, especially in regions like law enforcement, employing practices, and credit scoring. Addressing predisposition in calculations is fundamental to guarantee reasonableness and non-separation, lining up with standards of common freedoms.

Security and Digital Dangers:

The interconnected idea of arising advancements opens weaknesses to digital dangers and security breaks. Vindictive entertainers can take advantage of shortcomings in computer based intelligence frameworks, IoT gadgets, and blockchain networks, presenting dangers to people, associations, and, surprisingly, public safety. Safeguarding against digital dangers becomes principal to maintaining the right to security.

Independent Weapons and Moral Worries:

The advancement of independent weapons, controlled by artificial intelligence, raises moral worries about the utilization of deadly power without human intercession. The organization of such weapons moves the right to life and the standards of compassionate regulation. Finding some kind of harmony between military development and moral contemplations is essential to forestall the abuse of cutting edge innovations in furnished clashes.

Moral Systems and Basic liberties Securities:

Dependable simulated intelligence and Moral Rules:

Building dependable simulated intelligence frameworks expects adherence to moral rules that focus on straightforwardness, responsibility, and reasonableness. Moral systems, like the OECD's man-made intelligence Standards and the EU's Morals Rules for Dependable simulated intelligence, accentuate human-driven approaches and the security of key privileges. Coordinating moral contemplations into the plan and organization of man-made intelligence is fundamental for moderating possible damages.

Information Insurance Guidelines:

Information security guidelines, like the Overall Information Assurance Guideline (GDPR) in the European Association, lay out norms for the legal and moral handling of individual information. These guidelines engage people with command over their information and expect associations to carry out measures to safeguard security privileges. Reinforcing and extending such guidelines around the world is pivotal to tending to protection worries in the computerized time.

Basic liberties Effect Appraisals:

Directing Common freedoms Effect Appraisals (HRIAs) for arising innovations can help recognize and moderate possible dangers. HRIAs assess the effect of advances on basic liberties, taking into account factors like protection, non-separation, and the right to opportunity of articulation. Incorporating HRIAs into the advancement lifecycle guarantees that moral contemplations are implanted all along.

Worldwide Cooperation and Standards:

Laying out worldwide standards and cooperative structures is vital for address the worldwide idea of arising innovations. The improvement of standards, directed by basic freedoms standards, can make a mutual perspective of moral practices. Cooperative endeavors including legislatures, industry, common society, and the scholarly community cultivate a comprehensive way to deal with dealing with the moral difficulties presented by innovative headways.

Challenges in Execution:

Implementation and Responsibility:

Regardless of the presence of moral systems and guidelines, upholding them presents difficulties. The quick speed of mechanical development frequently dominates administrative measures. Furthermore, holding people, associations, or even legislatures responsible for infringement stays a perplexing errand, requiring facilitated endeavors and a pledge to enforceable guidelines.

Worldwide Abberations in Access and Effect:

The advantages and dangers related with arising advancements are not consistently conveyed internationally. Differences in admittance to innovation, computerized proficiency, and administrative structures add to an advanced gap. Crossing over these holes is fundamental to guarantee that the advantages of innovative progressions are shared comprehensively, lining up with the standards of equivalent open door and non-separation.

Potentially negative side-effects and Moral Issues:

Potentially negative side-effects of arising advances, whether as unexpected predispositions in artificial intelligence frameworks or accidental ecological effects, present continuous difficulties. Moral issues, for example, the utilization of artificial intelligence in decision-production with possibly life changing outcomes, require nuanced contemplations. Tending to these difficulties requests continuous reflection, flexibility, and a guarantee to iterative moral systems.

Basic liberties in the Period of Mechanical Development:

Computerized Citizenship and Strengthening:

Cultivating computerized citizenship is vital in guaranteeing that people are educated, enabled, and dynamic members in the advanced domain. Advancing computerized education, information proficiency, and attention to advanced freedoms engage people to capably explore the advanced scene. Computerized citizenship lines up with the standards of opportunity of articulation and admittance to data.

Tech for Good Drives:

Tech for Good drives embody endeavors to use innovation for positive social effect. Drives resolving issues, for example, environmental change, medical services access, and training disparity feature the capability of innovation to add to the acknowledgment of basic liberties. These drives feature the extraordinary force of innovation when lined up with moral standards and cultural prosperity

7.1 Impact of Technology on Human Rights

The significant and speeding up headways in innovation have changed essentially every part of current life, offering phenomenal open doors for progress and availability. In any case, as we explore this time of mechanical advancement, it becomes basic to examine the nuanced effect of innovation on common liberties. This investigation dives into the multilayered manners by which innovation both upgrades and difficulties the security and acknowledgment of crucial basic liberties.

Positive Effects:

Admittance to Data and Opportunity of Articulation:

Innovation, especially the web and virtual entertainment stages, has democratized admittance to data, engaging people to practice their right to opportunity of articulation. Online spaces give a stage to different voices, working with the trading of thoughts, encouraging community commitment, and testing conventional power structures. The capacity to offer viewpoints and access data universally has turned into a foundation of contemporary basic freedoms activism.

Worldwide Network and Correspondence:

The interconnectedness worked with by innovation has risen above geological limits, encouraging worldwide network and correspondence. Video conferencing, informal organizations, and texting stages empower people to impart across borders, advancing diverse exchange and world-wide cooperation. This interconnectedness adds to a feeling of worldwide fortitude, underscoring the comprehensiveness of common freedoms.

Progressions in Medical services and Biotechnology:

Mechanical developments in medical services and biotechnology have essentially worked on clinical diagnostics, therapies, and exploration. From telemedicine and wellbeing observing applications to leap forwards in hereditary examination, innovation improves the right to wellbeing. Distant medical care administrations, particularly important in the midst of worldwide wellbeing emergencies, give availability and inclusivity in medical services conveyance.

Training and Information Access:

Innovation has changed the scene of schooling, making information more open to assorted populaces. Web based learning stages, open instructive assets, and digital books empower people overall to get to instructive materials. This democratization of information adds to one side to training, encouraging long lasting learning valuable open doors and separating conventional obstructions to get to.

Difficulties and Adverse consequences:

Protection Disintegration and Observation:

The omnipresence of innovation has prompted an inescapable assort-ment of individual information, raising worries about security disinte-gration. Reconnaissance advancements, including facial acknowledgment frameworks and information mining, present dangers to one side to secu-rity. Legislatures and confidential substances' broad observation capaci-ties can encroach on people's independence, making a sensitive harmony between safety efforts and protecting security privileges.

Algorithmic Inclination and Separation:

Man-made intelligence calculations, while controlling various mechan-ical applications, can acquire and propagate predispositions present in preparing information. This algorithmic predisposition appears in biased results, influencing underestimated networks excessively. From one-sided recruiting cycles to law enforcement applications, the oppressive effect of innovation challenges the standards of non-separation and equivalent insurance under the law.

Network safety Dangers and Computerized Separation:

The interconnected idea of innovation uncovered people and social orders to network safety dangers. Cyberattacks, information breaks, and the weaponization of data present dangers to basic liberties, including the right to security and the right to opportunity of articulation. Additionally, the computerized partition - the hole between those with admittance to innovation and those without - fuels social disparities, restricting open doors for underestimated populaces.

Independent Weapons and Moral Quandaries:

The advancement of independent weapons, controlled by man-made intelligence, raises moral worries about the utilization of deadly power without human mediation. This provokes the right to life and standards of compassionate regulation. The moral difficulties encompassing independent weapons request cautious thought, worldwide participation, and lawful structures to forestall their abuse in furnished clashes.

Government Observation and Control:

Mass Observation Projects:

Legislatures overall have utilized mass observation programs, raising serious common liberties concerns. Programs like mass information assortment and observing of online exercises can smother opportunity of articulation, limit political dispute, and make a chilling impact on people's eagerness to practice their freedoms. Offsetting public safety interests with individual privileges stays a hostile test.

Social Credit Frameworks:

In specific purviews, the joining of innovation into administration has led to social credit frameworks. These frameworks use calculations to evaluate people's way of behaving, impacting admittance to administrations, travel, and work in light of a mathematical score. The potential for misuse and separation in such frameworks presents dangers to security, opportunity of development, and the option to work.

The Job of Partnerships and Advanced Stages:

Information Imposing business models and Double-dealing:

Innovation partnerships, frequently employing huge impact, gather tremendous measures of client information, raising worries about information syndications and double-dealing. The adaptation of individual information without informed assent difficulties people's command over their data. Administrative measures are fundamental to guarantee that companies focus on client privileges and stick to moral information rehearses.

Content Control and Opportunity of Articulation:

Advanced stages, as watchmen of online substance, face the test of offsetting content balance with the right to opportunity of appearance. Choices on what content to permit or eliminate can be abstract, prompting worries about restriction and predisposition. Finding some kind of harmony that forestalls the spread of unsafe substance while regarding assorted points of view stays a continuous test.

Administrative Reactions and Worldwide Participation:

Information Insurance Guidelines:

Perceiving the need to address security concerns, information insurance guidelines, like the GDPR in the European Association, set principles for the mindful treatment of individual information. These guidelines engage people with command over their data, requiring straightforwardness and responsibility from associations. Reinforcing and extending such guidelines internationally is urgent for safeguarding security privileges.

Man-made intelligence Morals and Rules:

Perceiving the moral difficulties presented by man-made intelligence, different substances have created rules to advance dependable artificial intelligence improvement. The OECD's simulated intelligence Standards and the EU's Morals Rules for Reliable man-made intelligence focus on human-driven approaches, straightforwardness, and responsibility. Complying with moral rules is fundamental to relieve the dangers related with man-made intelligence applications.

Global Common liberties System:

The worldwide basic freedoms structure, incorporating deals and shows, gives an establishment to tending to the effect of innovation on common liberties. Maintaining standards like the right to protection, opportunity of articulation, and non-separation, worldwide participation is critical to guarantee that mechanical headways line up with basic liberties norms.

Cultivating Moral Tech Development:

Moral Plan and Human-Driven Approaches:

Coordinating moral contemplations into the plan and advancement of innovation is fundamental for limiting adverse consequences. Human-driven approaches focus on client prosperity, security, and inclusivity, guaranteeing that innovation serves mankind instead of coincidentally hurting.

Public Mindfulness and Advanced Education:

Engaging people with advanced education and attention to their computerized privileges is essential. State funded instruction drives can improve comprehension of innovation's effect on common liberties, empowering people to settle on informed decisions, safeguard their protection, and supporter for moral tech rehearses.

7.2 Surveillance and Privacy Concerns

In the computerized age, the expansion of reconnaissance advances has become pervasive, offering the two open doors for improved security and presenting huge difficulties to individual protection. This investigation digs into the multifaceted connection among reconnaissance and protection, inspecting the advancing scene of observation innovations, their cultural ramifications, and the sensitive equilibrium that should be struck to shield key security privileges.

Development of Observation Advancements:

CCTV and Actual Reconnaissance:

Shut circuit TV (CCTV) frameworks address a longstanding type of reconnaissance, at first centered around open spaces and later extending to private premises. These frameworks, frequently utilized for wrongdoing avoidance and public wellbeing, have become basic to metropolitan foundation. Be that as it may, concerns emerge with respect to their possible abuse for mass observation and the disintegration of individual security.

Biometric Observation:

Progressions in biometric innovations, including facial acknowledgment and finger impression filtering, have introduced another period of reconnaissance abilities. Biometric information, once gathered, presents remarkable protection challenges because of its delicate nature. States and confidential elements progressively send biometric reconnaissance for different purposes, raising worries about exactness, assent, and the potential for biased results.

Web and Advanced Observation:

The digitization of correspondence and data has worked with broad advanced observation. Government offices and enterprises take part in mass information assortment, checking on the web exercises, and breaking down computerized correspondences. Issues of information security, the right to secrecy, and insurance against outlandish reconnaissance have become integral to conversations on computerized privileges.

Area Following and Versatile Reconnaissance:

Cell phones, outfitted with GPS innovation, empower unavoidable area following. States and specialist co-ops regularly access and store area information, apparently for purposes like public security and designated promoting. Be that as it may, the steady checking of people's developments raises significant security worries, as it reveals definite bits of knowledge into individual lives and schedules.

Security Concerns and Basic freedoms Suggestions:

Right to Security:

The right to security is a central basic liberty cherished in different peaceful accords and public constitutions. Security is characteristic for individual independence, individual flexibility, and the assurance of one's pride. Reconnaissance innovations, if uncontrolled, can infringe upon this right, prompting a chilling impact on opportunity of articulation and repressing people from practicing their freedoms unafraid of investigation.

Opportunity of Articulation and Affiliation:

Broad observation can dissuade people from unreservedly offering their viewpoints or taking part in political and social exercises. The apprehension about retaliation or separation in light of observation information might smother disagree and obstruct the development of affiliations that challenge winning standards. The intersection of reconnaissance and opportunity of articulation highlights the requirement for hearty security assurances.

Non-Segregation and Profiling:

Reconnaissance advances, especially those utilizing computerized reasoning, can coincidentally sustain predispositions and result in biased profiling. Facial acknowledgment frameworks, for instance, may show racial or orientation inclination, prompting vile ramifications for specific socioeconomics. Such unfair results present critical difficulties to the standards of non-segregation and equivalent assurance under the law.

Potential for Maltreatment of Force:

The brought together control and amassing of reconnaissance information present the gamble of maltreatment of force by states or elements using observation abilities. Designated reconnaissance of political protesters, minorities, or activists can prompt denials of basic liberties and subvert majority rule standards. The potential for uncontrolled observation to think power and smother resistance requires rigid balanced governance.

Government Reconnaissance and Common Freedoms:

Mass Reconnaissance Projects:

States, frequently for the sake of public safety, take part in mass observation programs that include the mass assortment of information for a huge scope. These projects, as uncovered by informants and insightful reporting, raise worries about the proportionality of reconnaissance measures and the effect on common freedoms. Adjusting the basic of safety with the insurance of individual privileges stays a mind boggling challenge.

Regulation and Legitimate Shields:

The lawful structures administering reconnaissance rehearses change across wards, with some giving hearty protections and oversight components, while others might have more lenient systems. Finding some kind of harmony between the requirement for powerful policing protecting individual security requires clear regulation, autonomous legal oversight, and instruments to consider specialists responsible for mishandles.

Corporate Observation and Information Abuse:

Information Adaptation and Profiling:

Enterprises regularly participate in reconnaissance for business purposes, gathering and dissecting client information to make nitty gritty profiles for designated promoting.

The commodification of individual information raises worries about informed assent, client independence, and the potential for abuse. People may accidentally exchange their security for admittance to computerized administrations, featuring the requirement for straightforwardness and moral information rehearses.

Virtual Entertainment and Social Observation:

Virtual entertainment stages, while offering roads for network, take part in broad conduct reconnaissance. Calculations investigate client collaborations, inclinations, and online way of behaving to tailor content and ads. The adaptation of client consideration and the control of client conduct for business gain highlight the requirement for straightforwardness, client control, and moral guidelines in the domain of web-based entertainment observation.

Observation With regards to General Wellbeing and Crises:

Pandemics and Contact Following:

General wellbeing crises, like the Coronavirus pandemic, have prompted the reception of reconnaissance measures for contact following and checking the spread of irresistible illnesses. While these actions are pointed toward defending general wellbeing, concerns emerge about the drawn out suggestions for protection, information maintenance, and the possible standardization of reconnaissance rehearses past the quick emergency.

Crisis Powers and Common Freedoms:

States might summon crisis powers during emergencies, conceding them more extensive observation capacities. While such measures might be considered significant for public wellbeing, they likewise increase the gamble of misuses and disintegration of common freedoms. Finding some kind of harmony between answering crises and maintaining essential privileges requires clear legitimate structures and intermittent reassessment of crisis measures.

Defensive Measures and Moral Contemplations:

Encryption and Advanced Security:

The utilization of encryption innovations can improve advanced security and safeguard correspondences from outlandish observation. Encryption, when carried out really, guarantees that main approved gatherings can get to delicate data, reinforcing the right to private correspondence. Notwithstanding, discusses persevere about the harmony between security needs and the difficulties presented by encoded interchanges for policing.

Moral Plan and Straightforwardness:

Inserting moral contemplations into the plan of observation advances is fundamental for alleviating protection gambles.

Straightforward plan rehearses, client assent instruments, and clear correspondence about information assortment and use upgrade responsibility. Moral rules ought to focus on limiting mischief, forestalling unfair results, and maintaining the standards of common freedoms.

Public Mindfulness and Backing:

Computerized Proficiency and Protection Instruction:

Enabling people with advanced proficiency and security instruction is pivotal for cultivating attention to reconnaissance gambles and defensive measures. Computerized proficiency drives can assist people with settling on informed decisions about their internet based exercises, comprehend the ramifications of information sharing, and promoter for security privileges.

Backing for Protection Freedoms:

Common society associations and security advocates assume an essential part in considering states and companies responsible for observation rehearses. Promotion endeavors center around molding public talk, testing meddlesome reconnaissance measures, and pushing for administrative changes that reinforce security insurances. A watchful common society is fundamental for keeping up with the fragile harmony among security and protection.

7.3 Technological Solutions to Human Rights Challenges

The fast development of innovation holds monstrous potential for tending to complex basic liberties challenges. As social orders wrestle with issues going from disparity and segregation to admittance to instruction and medical services, creative innovative arrangements have arisen as integral assets for positive change. This investigation digs into the crossing point of innovation and common liberties, inspecting the groundbreaking effect of different mechanical arrangements and the moral contemplations that go with their execution.

Admittance to Data and Computerized Incorporation:

Web Availability and Computerized Admittance:

Crossing over the computerized partition is a basic move toward guaranteeing evenhanded admittance to data and engaging underestimated networks. Drives pointed toward extending web availability, for example, satellite-based internet providers and local area Wi-Fi projects, add to advanced consideration. These endeavors cultivate admittance to instructive assets, open positions, and data fundamental for community cooperation, lining up with the standards of opportunity of data.

Internet Learning Stages and Instructive Correspondence:

Innovation has reformed training, offering web based learning stages that rise above geological hindrances. E-learning drives, particularly in underserved locales, give admittance to quality schooling. Gigantic Open Internet based Courses (MOOCs) and advanced instructive assets upgrade instructive balance, engaging people to obtain abilities and information independent of their area or financial foundation.

Medical care Developments and Telemedicine:

Telemedicine and Distant Medical care:

Telemedicine use innovation to beat geological limitations and further develop medical services availability. Virtual conferences, remote checking, and telehealth stages work with clinical consideration conveyance, particularly in remote or underserved regions. Telemedicine adds to one side to wellbeing by improving patient access, decreasing medical services variations, and giving ideal clinical intercessions.

Wellbeing Information Investigation for General Wellbeing:

High level information examination and man-made reasoning assume a urgent part in tending to general wellbeing challenges. Breaking down wellbeing information, including examples of sicknesses and medical care results, empowers more powerful asset allotment and proactive wellbeing intercessions. These innovations engage legislatures and medical care associations to go with informed choices, adding to one side to wellbeing for whole populaces.

Compassionate Advances in Emergency Reaction:

Satellite Symbolism for Catastrophe Alleviation:

Satellite symbolism and geospatial advancements have demonstrated significant in catastrophe reaction and helpful endeavors. During catastrophic events or clashes, ongoing satellite information supports surveying the degree of harm, planning aid projects, and guaranteeing the wellbeing of impacted populaces. These advancements improve the right to life by working with quick and designated reactions in emergency circumstances.

Blockchain for Straightforward Guide Dissemination:

Blockchain innovation brings straightforwardness and responsibility into philanthropic guide dissemination. By utilizing decentralized records, blockchain guarantees that help exchanges are secure, discernible, and impervious to extortion. This development tends to difficulties like debasement and bungle, adding to the productive and moral appropriation of compassionate help.

Progressions in Biotechnology and Hereditary Exploration:

Accuracy Medication and Customized Medical services:

Biotechnological headways, especially in genomics, have prepared for accuracy medication. Fitting clinical medicines to a person's hereditary cosmetics upgrades treatment viability and decreases unfavorable impacts. Accuracy medication lines up with the right to wellbeing by giving customized medical care arrangements, tending to explicit hereditary elements that impact infection vulnerability and therapy reactions.

Quality Altering and Moral Contemplations:

Advancements like CRISPR-Cas9 have introduced opportunities for quality altering, raising moral contemplations about the alteration of human genomes. While these advances hold guarantee for treating hereditary issues, worries about unseen side-effects, moral oversight, and the potential for creator infants require cautious guideline and moral rules.

Artificial intelligence and Information driven Arrangements:

Artificial intelligence in Prescient Policing and Predisposition Alleviation:

Man-made brainpower is used in prescient policing to break down wrongdoing designs and improve policing. In any case, worries about predisposition in artificial intelligence calculations and unfair results have provoked endeavors to alleviate predispositions. Moral man-made intelligence systems and continuous examination plan to guarantee that prescient policing advancements maintain the standards of non-segregation and equivalent insurance under the law.

Information driven Ways to deal with Tackle Imbalance:

Tackling the force of information investigation takes into consideration proof based policymaking to address fundamental imbalances. Information driven approaches recognize differences in regions like schooling, work, and medical services, empowering states and associations to execute designated mediations. Moral contemplations incorporate shielding security and guaranteeing that information driven strategies don't compound existing disparities.

Blockchain for Decentralized Character and Security:

Decentralized Character Frameworks:

Blockchain innovation offers answers for upgrade character the board and safeguard people's security. Decentralized character frameworks empower clients to control and validate their own data without dependence on concentrated specialists. This tends to protection concerns related with customary character frameworks, cultivating client independence and lining up with the right to security.

Blockchain in Production network Straightforwardness:

Blockchain's straightforwardness and unchanging nature make it a useful asset for guaranteeing moral stock chains. Following the beginning and excursion of items, particularly in enterprises like style and horticulture, permits shoppers to go with informed decisions. This innovation advances responsibility, lessens abuse, and adds to one side to fair working circumstances.

Challenges and Moral Contemplations:

Advanced Freedoms and Security Concerns:

The expanded dependence on innovation raises worries about advanced freedoms and security. Adjusting the advantages of mechanical arrangements with the assurance of individual security requires hearty lawful systems, straightforwardness, and components to address information breaks. Finding some kind of harmony is fundamental for maintaining the right to protection in an interconnected advanced scene.

Moral computer based intelligence Improvement and Inclination Alleviation:

The turn of events and sending of man-made intelligence request moral contemplations to forestall predisposition and separation. Executing rules for moral simulated intelligence advancement, including straightforwardness, responsibility, and inclusivity, is urgent. Nonstop observing and change of calculations to alleviate inclination guarantee that artificial intelligence innovations contribute decidedly to basic liberties without building up existing disparities.

Chapter 8

Future Trends and Challenges

As we stand at the slope of a future molded by fast innovative headways, the convergence of common freedoms and innovation presents a perplexing and dynamic scene. The ceaseless advancement of computerized instruments, man-made consciousness, biotechnology, and availability offers remarkable chances to address worldwide difficulties. Be that as it may, this future isn't without its considerable difficulties. This investigation dives into the arising patterns and intricacies that will shape the nexus between basic freedoms and innovation, and the basic of exploring these elements for an additional fair and impartial world.

Arising Patterns in Innovation and Basic liberties:

Headways in Man-made reasoning (computer based intelligence):

The direction of simulated intelligence improvement is ready to achieve groundbreaking changes in different areas. AI calculations, profound brain organizations, and normal language handling are developing quickly, offering prospects in medical care diagnostics, customized training, and prescient examination. In any case, the moral ramifications, likely predispositions, and the requirement for responsibility in artificial intelligence dynamic cycles stay basic difficulties.

Biotechnology and Genomic Altering:

Biotechnological headways, especially in genomic altering devices like CRISPR-Cas9, hold guarantees for treating hereditary illnesses and improving human abilities. The capacity to alter qualities, nonetheless, raises moral predicaments encompassing fashioner children, potentially negative results, and fair admittance to these innovations. Finding some kind of harmony among development and moral contemplations is basic coming soon for biotechnology.

The Web of Things (IoT) and Availability:

The expansion of interconnected gadgets through IoT is making a hyper-associated world. Brilliant urban communities, wearable gadgets, and IoT-empowered foundation offer exceptional information assortment abilities. While these innovations upgrade proficiency and comfort, they raise worries about protection, security, and the potential for mass observation. Offsetting network with security shields will be an essential test from here on out.

Blockchain Innovation and Decentralization:

Blockchain's decentralized and secure nature has applications past digital currency. It offers opportunities for straightforward stockpile chains, decentralized personality frameworks, and secure information sharing. Notwithstanding, challenges connected with adaptability, energy utilization, and administrative structures should be addressed for blockchain to live up to its true capacity in guaranteeing straightforwardness and responsibility.

Challenges at the Crossing point of Innovation and Basic liberties:

Protection Disintegration and Reconnaissance State:

The unavoidable assortment of individual information in the computerized age raises worries about protection disintegration and the potential for a reconnaissance state. States and enterprises bridle information for different purposes, from designated promoting to policing. Finding some kind of harmony between utilizing information for cultural advantages and safeguarding individual protection privileges is a squeezing challenge for what's in store.

Algorithmic Predisposition and Separation:

As computer based intelligence calculations assume an undeniably compelling part in dynamic cycles, tending to algorithmic predisposition becomes significant. Predisposition in calculations, whether in employing rehearses, law enforcement frameworks, or monetary appraisals, can sustain existing disparities. Creating moral man-made intelligence systems, guaranteeing different portrayal in computer based intelligence improvement, and cultivating straightforwardness are fundamental to relieve predisposition.

Computerized Imbalance and Access Abberations:

The computerized partition continues all around the world, with variations in admittance to innovation, advanced education, and online assets. Overcoming this issue is essential to guarantee that the advantages of innovative progressions are comprehensive.

Future endeavors ought to zero in on improving advanced foundation, advancing moderateness, and giving evenhanded admittance to instructive and financial open doors.

Moral Ramifications of Biotechnology:

As biotechnology progresses, the moral contemplations encompassing hereditary altering, cloning, and bioengineering become more mind boggling. Inquiries of assent, unseen side-effects, and the potential for making planner people require strong moral structures and worldwide participation. Guaranteeing that biotechnological developments line up with common freedoms standards is a diverse test.

Security Dangers and Online protection Difficulties:

The interconnected idea of innovation opens social orders to online protection dangers. Malevolent entertainers, state-supported etc., can take advantage of weaknesses in basic framework, prompting information breaks, financial disturbances, and dangers to public safety. Reinforcing network safety measures, global collaboration, and creating strong computerized foundation are principal challenges for what's in store.

Future Headings in Common freedoms and Innovation:

Upgrading Computerized Proficiency and Training:

Cultivating computerized proficiency becomes fundamental for exploring the complexities of the advanced scene. Schooling systems should adjust to outfit people with the abilities to basically survey data, grasp the ramifications of innovation on common freedoms, and connect capably in the advanced circle. Enabling people through training is a foundation for future common freedoms promotion.

Worldwide Administration and Administrative Systems:

The worldwide idea of innovation requests cooperative administration systems. Legislatures, worldwide associations, and the confidential area need to cooperate to lay out administrative norms that safeguard basic liberties. Peaceful accords, shows, and deals should adjust to the difficulties presented by arising advancements, guaranteeing that moral contemplations are implanted in lawful structures.

Moral Plan and Mindful Advancement:

The standards of moral plan and mindful advancement will be central in molding the eventual fate of innovation. From computer based intelligence improvement to biotechnological headways, integrating moral contemplations at the plan stage is urgent. Tech organizations, scientists, and trend-setters should focus on basic liberties standards, straightforwardness, and responsibility to forestall unseen side-effects.

Common Society Commitment and Support:

Common society assumes a critical part in considering legislatures and enterprises responsible for their activities at the crossing point of innovation and basic freedoms. Backing gatherings, NGOs, and basic freedoms safeguards need to effectively take part in molding approaches, bringing issues to light, and requesting responsibility. A careful common society guarantees that innovative progressions line up with the standards of equity, uniformity, and human respect.

Moral Contemplations in Mechanical Development:

Informed Assent and Client Independence:

As innovation progressively collaborates with individual information, guaranteeing informed assent and client independence becomes basic. People ought to have command over how their information is gathered, utilized, and shared. Developments in biotechnology, simulated intelligence, and different fields should focus on straightforward correspondence and regard for individual decisions.

Algorithmic Straightforwardness and Responsibility:

Calculations affecting dynamic cycles should be straightforward and responsible. Understanding how calculations work, the information they use, and the potential inclinations they might present is fundamental for building trust. Integrating components for inspecting, making sense of computer based intelligence choices, and giving roads to claim are pivotal strides toward algorithmic responsibility.

8.1 Anticipated Changes in Human Rights Landscape

As we peer into the future, the basic liberties scene is ready for extraordinary changes driven by a conversion of international movements, mechanical progressions, and cultural turns of events. The developing elements present an intricate embroidery of difficulties and potential open doors that will shape the manner in which social orders defend and advance basic freedoms. This investigation dives into the expected changes in the common liberties scene, tending to key subjects like worldwide administration, mechanical effects, civil rights developments, and the basic of flexibility despite a quickly developing world.

Worldwide Administration and Common liberties:

Changes in International Power:

Expected changes in the conveyance of international power are probably going to impact the worldwide basic liberties plan.

As arising powers champion themselves on the world stage, there might be shifts in needs, coalitions, and conciliatory techniques. This can affect the adequacy of worldwide organizations and joint efforts, requesting versatility in tending to basic freedoms challenges inside advancing international elements.

Change and Fortifying of Worldwide Establishments:

The requirement for a more hearty worldwide system to address worldwide difficulties is probably going to drive changes in existing organizations. Reinforcing bodies like the Assembled Countries (UN) and its specific offices might include returning to structures, improving responsibility systems, and advancing cooperation among countries. A revived obligation to multilateralism will be critical for tending to transnational basic freedoms issues.

Rise of New Basic liberties Plans:

Expected changes might deliver new basic freedoms plans reflecting developing cultural qualities and needs. Issues like ecological privileges, computerized freedoms, and the freedoms of weak populaces might acquire conspicuousness. The worldwide local area is probably going to wrestle with characterizing and safeguarding privileges in arising settings, requiring flexibility in lawful systems and support methodologies.

Innovative Effects on Common liberties:

Moral Contemplations in Computerized reasoning (man-made intelligence):

The rising joining of man-made intelligence into different parts of society raises significant moral contemplations. Expected changes remember a developing accentuation for dependable simulated intelligence improvement, straightforwardness in calculations, and endeavors to relieve predispositions. Basic freedoms systems should adjust to guarantee the moral arrangement of computer based intelligence advances, particularly in regions like business, law enforcement, and medical care.

Biotechnology and Hereditary Protection:

Propels in biotechnology, including quality altering and customized medication, present difficulties to hereditary security. The expected development in hereditary information accessibility might require vigorous guidelines to safeguard people from hereditary separation, unapproved utilization of hereditary data, and potential moral worries encompassing hereditary adjustments. Offsetting logical advancement with moral contemplations will be significant.

Computerized Freedoms and Security Insurance:

The rising digitization of day to day existence raises worries about computerized freedoms and protection. Expected changes remember an uplifted concentration for information insurance, network protection, and people's command over their computerized personalities. Legislatures, enterprises, and common society should team up to lay out and authorize vigorous legitimate structures that protect advanced privileges in a time of unavoidable mechanical network.

Civil rights Developments and Common liberties Backing:

Multifacetedness and Comprehensive Backing:

Civil rights developments are probably going to advance towards more diverse methodologies, perceiving the interconnectedness of different types of segregation and mistreatment. Expected changes include expanded accentuation on comprehensive backing that tends to the exceptional difficulties looked by people at the crossing points of race, orientation, sexuality, and other personality markers. Basic liberties support should adjust to guarantee an extensive and interconnected approach.

Computerized Activism and Worldwide Fortitude:

The computerized time has reshaped the scene of activism, empowering worldwide availability and preparation. Expected changes incorporate an intensification of advanced activism, outfitting the force of virtual entertainment, online stages, and innovation for basic liberties causes. Worldwide fortitude developments are probably going to arise, rising above boundaries and encouraging an aggregate reaction to common freedoms infringement on a worldwide scale.

Freedoms of Weak Populaces:

Expected changes in the common liberties scene remember an elevated concentration for the freedoms of weak populaces. This incorporates exiles, travelers, native networks, and those impacted by struggle or helpful emergencies. Basic liberties support should adjust to address the special difficulties looked by these populaces, guaranteeing their voices are heard and their privileges secured.

Environmental Change and Natural Freedoms:

Acknowledgment of Ecological Freedoms:

The heightening effects of environmental change are expected to lift the acknowledgment of ecological privileges as major common freedoms. Legislatures and global bodies might have to adjust their arrangements to address the freedoms of networks impacted by ecological debasement. This incorporates the right to a solid climate, admittance to clean water, and security from the unfriendly impacts of environmental change.

Lawful Systems for Natural Assurance:

The expected changes in the basic freedoms scene include the turn of events and reinforcing of legitimate structures for ecological assurance. Peaceful accords, public regulations, and legal instruments should adjust to consider states and enterprises responsible for ecological infringement. Natural equity will become essential to the more extensive basic freedoms talk.

Versatile Legitimate Systems and Insurances:

Joining of Arising Freedoms:

The expected changes in the basic liberties scene might require the consolidation of arising privileges that line up with advancing cultural standards. This incorporates privileges connected with arising advances, social movements, and the developing comprehension of human respect. Legitimate structures should adjust to really perceive and safeguard these arising freedoms.

Upgraded Requirement Instruments:

Reinforcing authorization components for common liberties assurances is an expected change because of advancing difficulties. This includes enabling worldwide common liberties bodies, guaranteeing consistence with basic freedoms deals, and considering violators responsible. Flexibility in requirement systems is urgent to address arising dangers to common liberties successfully.

8.2 Global Trends Shaping Responses to Human Rights

In the perplexing trap of international, mechanical, and cultural movements, worldwide reactions to common freedoms issues are constantly developing. A nuanced comprehension of the transaction between different patterns is essential for molding powerful reactions that address the mind boggling difficulties confronting the common freedoms scene. This investigation digs into key worldwide patterns molding reactions to basic liberties, enveloping international elements, mechanical progressions, civil rights developments, and the basic of encouraging global cooperation.

International Elements and Common freedoms:

Ascent of Dictatorship versus Majority rule Versatility:

One of the characterizing worldwide patterns molding reactions to basic freedoms is the continuous pressure between the ascent of dictator systems and the versatility of majority rule values. Tyrant legislatures, described by unified power, limitations on common freedoms, and a negligence for basic liberties, present difficulties to the global common freedoms system. The reaction to this pattern includes reinforcing vote based establishments, supporting for law and order, and encouraging global unions that maintain common freedoms standards.

Patriotism and Its Effect:

The resurgence of patriotism in different regions of the planet has suggestions for common freedoms reactions. Nationalistic plans frequently focus on the interests of a specific gathering, possibly underestimating minority networks and cultivating exclusionary strategies.

Neutralizing this pattern requires advancing comprehensive administration, pushing for minority privileges, and cultivating a worldwide talk that stresses the all inclusiveness of basic liberties past public boundaries.

Innovative Progressions and Basic freedoms:

Computerized Observation and Protection Concerns:

The fast extension of advanced observation innovations presents difficulties to one side to protection. States and companies bridle information for reconnaissance purposes, raising worries about mass information assortment, facial acknowledgment, and the disintegration of individual security. Answering this pattern requires the improvement of strong legitimate systems, peaceful accords on computerized privileges, and promotion for security assurances in the advanced age.

Man-made reasoning and Responsibility:

The reconciliation of computerized reasoning (computer based intelligence) into different aspects of life presents intricacies in responsibility. Algorithmic dynamic in regions like law enforcement, work, and medical services might sustain predispositions and result in unjustifiable results. Tending to this pattern requires laying out moral rules for man-made intelligence advancement, guaranteeing straightforwardness in calculations, and creating components for responsibility when man-made intelligence situation influence basic freedoms.

Civil rights Developments and Backing:

Ascent of Grassroots Developments:

Civil rights developments, driven by grassroots activism, are affecting reactions to basic freedoms issues. Developments like People of color Matter, #MeToo, and environment activism feature the force of aggregate activity in upholding for equity and fairness. Perceiving the significance of these developments includes enhancing underestimated voices, supporting city commitment, and incorporating grassroots points of view into strategy reactions.

Youth Activism and Intergenerational Cooperation:

An outstanding pattern forming basic freedoms reactions is the flood in youth activism. Youngsters are at the front of developments tending to environmental change, firearm savagery, and fundamental imbalances. Encouraging intergenerational joint effort is essential, perceiving the novel viewpoints and energy that youthful activists bring to common liberties support. Supporting youth-drove drives and incorporating their voices into dynamic cycles add to a more comprehensive methodology.

Global Cooperation and Multilateralism:

Difficulties to Multilateralism:

Worldwide reactions to basic liberties issues are impacted by difficulties to multilateralism. The ascent of unilateralism and suspicion towards worldwide foundations subvert cooperative endeavors. Tending to this pattern includes reaffirming the significance of multilateralism, fortifying worldwide foundations, and encouraging participation among countries to handle transnational common liberties challenges.

Job of Non-State Entertainers:

Non-state entertainers, including global companies, non-legislative associations (NGOs), and transnational promotion organizations, assume an undeniably huge part in forming common freedoms reactions. The pattern includes perceiving the effect of non-state entertainers on basic liberties, considering organizations responsible for moral practices, and utilizing the impact of common society in pushing for positive change.

Ecological Changes and Basic freedoms:

Environment Emergency and Weak People group:

The heightening environment emergency represents a danger to basic freedoms, especially for weak networks. Rising ocean levels, outrageous climate occasions, and asset consumption lopsidedly influence minimized populaces. Reactions to this pattern involve incorporating natural equity into basic liberties talk, pushing for environment activity, and guaranteeing that environment approaches focus on the freedoms of impacted networks.

Uprooting and Exile Freedoms:

Natural changes, combined with struggle and political shakiness, add to constrained removal and displaced person emergencies. Answering this pattern includes reinforcing worldwide exile security components, tending to the main drivers of relocation, and pushing for the freedoms of outcasts and uprooted people inside an exhaustive basic liberties system.

Monetary Imbalances and Basic liberties:

Worldwide Monetary Inconsistencies:

Monetary imbalances persevere universally, impacting reactions to basic liberties. The grouping of abundance and assets in specific locales worsens differences in admittance to schooling, medical care, and fundamental requirements. Tending to this pattern requires arrangements that focus on financial inclusivity, fair dispersion of assets, and endeavors to lift weak networks out of destitution.

Work Privileges and Innovative Disturbance:

Mechanical headways and mechanization influence work markets, raising worries about work uprooting and the disintegration of work freedoms. Answering this pattern includes reexamining work regulations, guaranteeing the security of laborers in the gig economy, and cultivating discourse between legislatures, organizations, and trade guilds to adjust to the changing idea of work.

Pandemics and Worldwide Wellbeing Concerns:

Pandemic Readiness and Wellbeing Value:

The Coronavirus pandemic has highlighted the significance of worldwide wellbeing reactions and the requirement for impartial admittance to medical care. Expected changes include focusing on pandemic readiness, guaranteeing fair conveyance of immunizations and clinical assets, and tending to the financial effects of wellbeing emergencies inside a basic freedoms structure.

Infodemics and Falsehood:

The infodemic going with wellbeing emergencies, portrayed by the quick spread of deception, represents a test to general wellbeing and common liberties. Answering this pattern requires powerful correspondence methodologies, media education drives, and global cooperation to counter falsehood while regarding opportunity of articulation.

8.3 Ongoing Challenges and Potential Solutions

While progress has been made in the domain of common liberties, continuous difficulties persevere, requiring a thorough assessment of expected arrangements. This investigation digs into the multi-layered moves that keep on obstructing the full acknowledgment of common liberties worldwide and proposes possible answers for cultivate positive change. From international intricacies to financial incongruities, the excursion towards an existence where basic freedoms are generally regarded requires purposeful endeavors and imaginative methodologies.

International Difficulties:

Dictatorship and Disintegration of Popularity based Values:

The ascent of dictator systems represents a huge test to common freedoms, portrayed by limitations on common freedoms, concealment of contradiction, and disintegration of vote based values.

To address this, the worldwide local area should fortify strategic instruments and multilateral organizations that maintain vote based standards. Participating in discourse with nations where basic liberties are under danger and advancing majority rule administration can act as proactive advances.

Patriotism and Exclusionary Strategies:

The resurgence of patriotism has brought about exclusionary approaches that minimize minority gatherings. A potential arrangement includes cultivating worldwide joint efforts that stress the common obligation of safeguarding basic liberties. Advancing social trade, instructive projects, and drives that praise variety can check the troublesome effect of patriot plans.

Innovative Difficulties:

Computerized Reconnaissance and Protection Infringement:

The development of computerized observation raises worries about security infringement and unrestrained government reconnaissance. To address this, legislatures should establish and uphold vigorous protection regulations that line up with global common freedoms principles. Furthermore, encouraging public mindfulness and commitment on advanced privileges is pivotal, enabling people to advocate for their protection in the computerized age.

Moral Difficulties in artificial intelligence and Biotechnology:

The moral ramifications of man-made brainpower and biotechnology require proactive measures. Laying out complete moral rules for computer based intelligence and biotechnological headways, including rigid oversight systems, is fundamental. Advancing interdisciplinary joint efforts between technologists, ethicists, and policymakers can guarantee that these innovations line up with common liberties standards.

Financial Variations:

Worldwide Monetary Imbalances:

Tenacious monetary imbalances ruin the acknowledgment of social and financial privileges. An answer includes executing strategies that address abundance inconsistencies, for example, moderate tax collection, social wellbeing nets, and comprehensive financial improvement techniques. Empowering capable strategic policies and fair exchange can add to additional evenhanded worldwide financial frameworks.

Work Privileges Even with Robotization:

The interruption brought about by innovative progressions, especially robotization, presents difficulties to work privileges. Arrangements incorporate rethinking and refreshing work regulations to oblige developing work structures.

Advancing professional preparation and reskilling projects can enable laborers to explore the changing position scene. Social exchange including states, bosses, and laborers is significant to work out some kind of harmony between mechanical advancement and work privileges.

Worldwide Wellbeing and Ecological Worries:

Pandemics and Evenhanded Medical services Access:

The Coronavirus pandemic has featured differences in medical care access. To address this, there is a requirement for worldwide collaboration in immunization conveyance, guaranteeing that all nations have evenhanded access. Reinforcing medical care foundation, supporting examination on irresistible sicknesses, and cultivating worldwide cooperation in general wellbeing endeavors are fundamental parts of an extensive arrangement.

Natural Debasement and Common liberties:

Natural debasement lopsidedly influences weak networks, compromising their privileges to life, wellbeing, and vocation. A comprehensive arrangement includes coordinating ecological equity into common freedoms systems. States and partnerships should be considered responsible for ecological infringement, and approaches advancing reasonable improvement ought to be focused on. Engaging people group to partake in ecological dynamic cycles is basic to guaranteeing their freedoms are secured.

Civil rights Goals:

Comprehensive Ways to deal with Battle Segregation:

Segregation in view of race, orientation, sexual direction, or different personalities stays an unavoidable test. Comprehensive schooling, mindfulness crusades, and regulative measures are significant in battling segregation. Advancing variety in positions of authority and enhancing underestimated voices through media portrayal add to encouraging comprehensive social orders.

Youth Strengthening and Municipal Commitment:

Bridling the energy of youth activism requires making roads for significant municipal commitment. Integrating municipal training into school educational plans, supporting youth-drove drives, and giving stages to youthful voices in dynamic cycles are essential arrangements. States and associations should perceive the organization of youngsters as dynamic supporters of forming a fair and evenhanded society.

Helpful Emergencies and Constrained Uprooting:

Exile Freedoms and Global Collaboration:

Tending to the difficulties looked by exiles requests global participation. Arrangements incorporate reinforcing global outcast security instruments, giving helpful guide, and tending to the underlying drivers of relocation. Advancing exchange and joint effort between have nations, contributor countries, and helpful associations is fundamental to guaranteeing the privileges and pride of exiles are maintained.

Compromise and Peacebuilding:

Persevering contentions add to common freedoms infringement for a monstrous scope. Practical arrangements include strategic endeavors to determine clashes, support for peacebuilding drives, and responsibility for atrocities. Worldwide associations and peacekeeping powers should be engaged to assume a proactive part in forestalling and settling clashes.

Chapter 9

Conclusion

In the perplexing embroidery of international movements, mechanical headways, and diligent cultural difficulties, the excursion towards a reality where common freedoms are generally maintained requests relentless responsibility, flexibility, and imaginative arrangements. As we ponder the continuous difficulties and potential arrangements framed, it becomes clear that the mission for common freedoms rises above disconnected endeavors and requires a cooperative, comprehensive methodology. This end tries to integrate the key subjects examined, stressing the interconnectedness of different difficulties and the basic of encouraging a worldwide ethos that places human pride at its center.

Interconnected Difficulties:

The assessment of progressing difficulties uncovers a multifaceted web where international intricacies, innovative issues, financial variations, and ecological worries converge. Tyranny, patriotism, and exclusionary strategies entwine with computerized reconnaissance, moral worries in computer based intelligence, and financial disparities, framing a nexus of difficulties that requires nuanced reactions. Perceiving these interconnections is major to forming exhaustive arrangements that address the complex idea of basic freedoms issues.

The Job of Worldwide Collaboration:

A common subject in tending to difficulties is the critical job of worldwide participation and multilateralism. Whether battling dictatorship, controlling innovative headways, or answering worldwide wellbeing emergencies, cooperative endeavors arise as key parts of viable arrangements. Reinforcing worldwide organizations, cultivating political discourse, and advancing a common obligation regarding basic freedoms insurance are basic parts of a forward-looking methodology. In reality as we know it where difficulties rise above borders, the obligation to aggregate activity becomes basic.

Innovative Moral Contemplations:

The fast development of innovation presents moral contemplations that influence the actual texture of common liberties. As computerized reasoning and biotechnology become progressively coordinated into our lives, moral rules, straightforwardness, and responsibility arise as essential support points for protecting basic liberties. Finding some kind of harmony between mechanical development and moral contemplations requires a purposeful exertion from policymakers, technologists, and society at large. The arrangements lie in encouraging interdisciplinary joint efforts, powerful administrative structures, and a moral establishment that places basic liberties at the cutting edge of mechanical headways.

Comprehensive Civil rights Developments:

The ascent of grassroots civil rights developments, frequently drove by youth activism, mirrors a worldwide longing for equity, value, and consideration. Perceiving the interesting force of assorted voices is fundamental for destroying foundational segregation and guaranteeing that basic liberties are not conceptual goals but rather substantial real factors for all. Training, media portrayal, and comprehensive arrangements are key instruments in advancing civil rights. Engaging underestimated networks and enhancing their stories add to an additional impartial and simply world.

Ecological Maintainability and Common liberties:

The lacing of ecological supportability with common liberties underlines the complicated connection between the prosperity of the planet and the poise of people. As environmental change compounds weaknesses, tending to ecological corruption becomes inseparable from safeguarding common liberties. The arrangements include incorporating natural equity into basic liberties systems, considering substances responsible for environmental infringement, and encouraging maintainable practices. Despite existential ecological difficulties, the quest for common liberties can't be separated from the basic of planetary stewardship.

Financial Inclusivity:

Financial differences persevere as a critical hindrance to the full acknowledgment of basic freedoms. Arrangements involve strategies that focus on monetary inclusivity, fair dispersion of assets, and the security of work freedoms despite innovative disturbance.

Maintainable improvement methodologies, dependable strategic policies, and worldwide collaboration in addressing monetary imbalances are essential to making social orders where people can flourish without being upset by fundamental financial variations.

Evacuee Freedoms and Compromise:

Helpful emergencies and constrained dislodging request an empathetic and composed reaction. Maintaining outcast freedoms requires fortifying worldwide insurance instruments as well as tending to the underlying drivers of dislodging through compromise and peacebuilding endeavors. The obligation to giving a noble life to those effectively dislodged highlights the worldwide local area's aggregate liability to safeguard the freedoms of the most helpless.

The Basic of Versatility:

As we explore the eventual fate of common liberties, flexibility arises as a principal basic. The powerful idea of difficulties, whether international, mechanical, or cultural, requires a methodology that advances pair with the evolving scene. Legitimate structures, conciliatory systems, and support philosophies should stay versatile to actually address arising basic liberties issues. A pledge to constant reflection, learning, and variation is fundamental for encouraging significant advancement.

Engaging Common Society and Grassroots Drives:

Common society, with its different cluster of non-legislative associations, activists, and supporters, assumes a urgent part in forming reactions to basic freedoms challenges. Enabling these elements, giving them the assets and stages to order change, is vital. The effect of grassroots drives, frequently drove by underestimated networks, supports the rule that significant advancement originates from the beginning. Perceiving the organization of people and networks to drive change guarantees that common freedoms support stays comprehensive and agent.

The Vision of a General Basic liberties Culture:

All in all, the quest for basic freedoms isn't an objective however a continuous excursion. It is an excursion towards a worldwide culture where the inborn respect of each and every individual isn't just perceived however effectively safeguarded and celebrated. The framed difficulties are impressive, yet they are not outlandish. The potential arrangements examined give a guide, underlining the requirement for aggregate responsibility, worldwide collaboration, and an unfaltering devotion to the standards revered in basic liberties instruments.

The vision of an existence where common freedoms are generally regarded requires a change in perspective in how social orders, states, and organizations approach their obligations. It requests a guarantee to equity, equity, and the acknowledgment that common liberties are natural, indissoluble, and reliant.

As we explore the intricacies representing things to come, let us stay conscious of the extraordinary force of aggregate activity, moral advancement, and the steadfast conviction that the acknowledgment of basic freedoms isn't simply a yearning however a basic for the prosperity and thriving of humankind.

9.1 Recap of Global Responses

In the complex domain of basic freedoms, the worldwide reactions to challenges looked by people and networks all over the planet are intelligent of the dynamic and interconnected nature of our globalized society. As we recap the broad investigation of worldwide reactions to common liberties issues, it becomes clear that the way toward an additional fair and impartial world requires a nuanced comprehension of the intricacies in question. This recap tries to combine the vital bits of knowledge and investigate the general subjects that have risen up out of the assessment of international, innovative, financial, and ecological difficulties, as well as the different methodologies utilized to address them.

International Elements:

The recap starts by returning to the international scene, where the ascent of tyranny and patriot feelings has presented huge difficulties to the all inclusive assurance of basic liberties. Across various areas, legislatures have wrestled with the fragile harmony between public interests and the basic to defend the privileges and poise, everything being equal. The reactions to these international difficulties highlight the significance of strategic commitment, worldwide collaboration, and the support for vote based values as fundamental parts of an aggregate work to protect and propel common freedoms on a worldwide scale.

Mechanical Progressions and Moral Contemplations:

In the computerized age, mechanical progressions have introduced the two potential open doors and difficulties for common freedoms. The recap dives into the moral contemplations encompassing man-made reasoning, biotechnology, and computerized reconnaissance. As the worldwide local area explores the moral predicaments presented by these advances, the all-encompassing reaction rotates around the foundation of hearty legitimate structures, moral rules, and peaceful accords that guarantee the dependable turn of events and arrangement of innovation. The accentuation on straightforwardness, responsibility, and the security of individual protection arises as a consistent idea in tending to the potential common liberties ramifications of mechanical advancement.

Financial Abberations:

Financial imbalances continue as a considerable test to the acknowledgment of social and monetary freedoms.

The recap features the worldwide reaction to these incongruities, underscoring the requirement for comprehensive monetary strategies, fair dissemination of assets, and the assurance of work freedoms. From addressing worldwide financial designs to adjusting to the changing idea of work, the accentuation is on cultivating a financial climate where all people have the chance to partake in a respectable way of life and admittance to fundamental administrations.

Ecological Worries and Basic liberties:

The crossing point of natural manageability and common freedoms arises as a basic subject in the recap. As the world wrestles with the effects of environmental change and natural debasement, the reactions highlight the need of incorporating ecological equity into common freedoms structures. From perceiving the privileges of networks impacted by natural emergencies to considering elements responsible for biological infringement, the worldwide local area is called upon to address the interconnected difficulties of ecological manageability and the insurance of principal basic freedoms.

Civil rights Developments:

The recap perceives the power and effect of civil rights developments, especially those drove by grassroots activism and youth commitment. Developments, for example, People of color Matter and environment activism highlight the meaning of aggregate activity in supporting for equity, correspondence, and foundational change. The worldwide reaction to these developments accentuates the significance of enhancing minimized voices, cultivating inclusivity, and recognizing the organization of people, particularly the adolescent, as impetuses for positive social change.

Global Participation and Multilateralism:

Worldwide collaboration and multilateralism arise as general subjects in the recap, cutting across different difficulties and reactions. Whether tending to international pressures, managing innovative headways, or answering worldwide wellbeing emergencies, the requirement for cooperative endeavors and reinforced global establishments is reliably underlined. The recap builds up the possibility that an aggregate obligation to maintaining common freedoms requires a unified front, where countries team up to address transnational difficulties and support the standards revered in global basic liberties instruments.

Strengthening of Common Society and Grassroots Drives:

The recap highlights the key job of common society, non-administrative associations (NGOs), and grassroots drives in forming reactions to basic liberties challenges. These elements act as imperative entertainers in upholding for change, enhancing underestimated voices, and considering states and organizations responsible. The recap features the significance of engaging common society as a vital system in encouraging a granular perspective to basic liberties backing, guaranteeing that the different requirements and viewpoints of networks are viewed as in molding reactions.

Flexibility and Nonstop Learning:
As the recap crosses through the different difficulties and reactions, a repetitive topic is the basic of versatility and consistent learning. The unique idea of common freedoms challenges, whether emerging from international movements, mechanical headways, or financial changes, requires a proactive and versatile methodology. The recap underlines the requirement for progressing reflection, learning, and the development of methodologies to really address arising common liberties issues in a quickly changing worldwide scene.

9.2 Call to Action for a Collective Effort
As we consider the far reaching investigation of worldwide reactions to common liberties issues, it is obvious that the difficulties looked by people and networks overall interest more than detached endeavors; they require an aggregate and deliberate worldwide reaction. This source of inspiration is a solicitation to states, common society, worldwide associations, and people the same, encouraging a common obligation to cultivate a worldwide culture where basic liberties are regarded on a fundamental level as well as effectively shielded practically speaking.

1. Building up the Groundwork of Worldwide Common freedoms:
   At the core of the source of inspiration is the revitalization of the basic standards revered in worldwide common freedoms instruments. Legislatures across the globe are encouraged to reaffirm their obligation to these instruments and effectively pursue their execution. The all inclusive nature of common liberties requests an aggregate affirmation that rises above international contrasts. Legislatures are called upon to coordinate basic liberties schooling into public educational programs, encouraging a culture where the consciousness of these freedoms turns into a fundamental piece of cultural qualities.

2. Reinforcing Worldwide Collaboration and Multilateralism:
   The source of inspiration underscores the basic of supporting global collaboration and multilateralism. In a period set apart by worldwide difficulties that rise above borders, countries are urged to participate in conciliatory endeavors that focus on exchange over strife. Cooperative drives, for example, joint exploration projects, social trades, and shared assets, can cultivate a climate where countries all things considered address basic freedoms challenges. Reinforcing worldwide organizations is critical, as they act as the bedrock for facilitated reactions to issues that influence the worldwide local area, from environmental change to pandemics.

3. Engaging Common Society and Grassroots Drives:
   Common society, non-administrative associations, and grassroots

drives are essential specialists chasing after basic liberties. This source of inspiration asks the worldwide local area to perceive and uphold the fundamental pretended by these substances.

Legislatures are urged to establish an empowering climate for common society to work unafraid of retaliation, cultivating a space where various voices can be heard. Monetary help, limit building, and cooperation among state run administrations and common society can enhance the effect of grassroots drives, guaranteeing that the worries and goals of networks are coordinated into strategy reactions.

4. Exploring the Moral Scene of Innovation:

As innovation keeps on advancing, moral contemplations become progressively central. This source of inspiration entreats legislatures, innovation engineers, and administrative bodies to cooperatively explore the moral scene of arising advancements. Laying out powerful moral rules, advancing straightforwardness in algorithmic navigation, and guaranteeing computerized protection are fundamental parts of this work. Peaceful accords that set moral norms for the turn of events and organization of innovation can make a blended methodology that focuses on common freedoms.

5. Tending to Financial Variations through Comprehensive Arrangements:

Financial variations persevere as a boundary to the full acknowledgment of common freedoms. This source of inspiration urges state run administrations to execute comprehensive monetary strategies that focus on fair circulation of assets. Moderate tax collection, social security nets, and drives to engage underestimated networks financially are fundamental systems. State run administrations, in a joint effort with the confidential area, are urged to embrace mindful strategic policies that add to feasible turn of events, fair work conditions, and social obligation.

6. Natural Equity as a Basic freedoms Basic:

Perceiving the inherent connection between natural manageability and common liberties, this source of inspiration advocates for a change in perspective towards ecological equity. States and companies are called upon to take on maintainable practices, limit natural effect, and be responsible for ecological infringement. Strategies that focus on the privileges of networks impacted by natural corruption, combined with worldwide joint effort to address environmental change, are fundamental stages towards a future where ecological equity is inseparable from the security of common liberties.

7. Advancing Civil rights through Incorporation:

Civil rights developments, frequently drove by grassroots activism and youth commitment, are instrumental in molding reactions to foundational disparities. This source of inspiration urges legislatures to pay attention to and draw in with these developments effectively. Strategies that advance inclusivity, variety, and equivalent portrayal are fundamental for destroying foundational segregation. By cultivating conditions where each person, no matter what their experience, is managed the cost of equivalent open doors, social orders can advance towards an additional fair and evenhanded future.

8. **Putting resources into Worldwide Wellbeing and Pandemic Readiness:**

The continuous worldwide wellbeing challenges, exemplified by the Coronavirus pandemic, highlight the requirement for expanded interest in worldwide wellbeing framework and pandemic readiness. This source of inspiration requires a cooperative work to guarantee impartial admittance to medical services assets, including immunizations, therapies, and clinical innovations. Legislatures, in organization with worldwide associations, are encouraged to focus on worldwide wellbeing as an aggregate liability, perceiving that the wellbeing and prosperity of people are basic parts of their innate common freedoms.

9. **Supporting for Exile Freedoms and Compromise:**

Tending to the predicament of exiles requires an aggregate obligation to compassionate qualities. State run administrations are called upon to fortify global displaced person security systems, offer help to have nations, and effectively take part in compromise and peacebuilding endeavors. By cultivating a climate where clashes are tended to strategically, and the freedoms of exiles are focused on, the worldwide local area can pursue an existence where constrained dislodging is limited, and the privileges of uprooted people are safeguarded.

10. **Obligation to Nonstop Learning and Flexibility:**

The source of inspiration finishes up with an accentuation on the obligation to persistent learning and flexibility. In a world that is continually developing, legislatures, associations, and people are encouraged to remain receptive to arising common freedoms challenges and proactively adjust their procedures. This responsibility includes encouraging a culture of contemplation, gaining from previous encounters, and embracing inventive ways to deal with address developing worldwide real factors.

9.3 Hope for a Better Future

In the midst of the intricacies and difficulties investigated in the thorough examination of worldwide reactions to basic liberties issues, there exists a significant wellspring of trust — an aggregate positive thinking that rises above lines, belief systems, and verifiable variations. This part is a thought of the groundbreaking likely intrinsic in the human soul and a dream for a future where the standards of common liberties are maintained as well as act as the foundation of a fair and evenhanded worldwide society.

1. The Force of Shared awareness:
   Trust exudes from the acknowledgment that the battle for basic freedoms isn't borne by confined people or countries yet is an aggregate undertaking that resounds across societies and ages. The worldwide cognizance, molded by shared upsides of equity, sympathy, and the inborn respect of each and every person, turns into a main thrust for positive change. It is inside this shared awareness that the seeds of trust are planted, growing into activities that rise above political, social, and financial boundaries.

2. Youth as Problem solvers:
   A huge wellspring of trust lies in the expanding activism of the young — a segment whose energy, enthusiasm, and obligation to equity have been impetuses for groundbreaking developments. From environment activism to civil rights crusades, the young have exhibited an enduring faith in the chance of a superior world. States and organizations are encouraged to effectively include and pay attention to the young, perceiving their organization as drivers of progress and overseers of a future where basic liberties are safeguarded as well as effectively supported.

3. Mechanical Development for Human Great:
   Notwithstanding moral quandaries presented by mechanical progressions, trust rises up out of the capability of development to be a power for good. States, tech ventures, and scientists can team up to tackle the extraordinary force of innovation in manners that line up with basic liberties standards. From involving man-made consciousness for social great to guaranteeing computerized protection, the confident vision is one where innovation turns into an empowering influence of common freedoms instead of a possible danger.

4. Grassroots Developments as Harbingers of Progress:
   Trust blooms in the grassroots developments that spring from the very networks impacted by basic freedoms challenges. Whether it be developments upholding for racial balance, orientation equity, or native freedoms, these natural drives are encouraging signs. State run

administrations and organizations are called upon to perceive, support, and intensify the voices of these developments, understanding that enduring change frequently starts at the grassroots level.

5. Multifaceted Fortitude:

The interconnectedness of the world encourages trust through diverse fortitude — an acknowledgment that the security of basic liberties is a common obligation. Legislatures, common society, and people are urged to embrace social variety and participate in discourse that rises above social contrasts. The expectation lies in the affirmation that in spite of different practices and chronicles, a common obligation to basic liberties can act as a binding together power.

6. Ecological Stewardship for People in the future:

Trust for a superior future is complicatedly connected to natural stewardship. Legislatures, partnerships, and people are encouraged to perceive the desperation of tending to environmental change and natural corruption. By embracing feasible works on, supporting sustainable power drives, and advocating natural equity, the expectation is to leave a livable planet for people in the future — an existence where the right to a spotless and solid climate is maintained.

7. Creative Discretion and Compromise:

In the domain of international affairs, trust lives in the potential for imaginative discretion and compromise. States are urged to move past conventional power elements and embrace exchange as an essential method for tending to questions. The expectation is for a reality where countries team up to find tranquil goals, perceiving that strategic arrangements add to the insurance of common freedoms on a worldwide scale.

8. Helpful Activity In the midst of Emergency:

Despite philanthropic emergencies, trust rises up out of the quick and sympathetic reaction of states, worldwide associations, and people. The arrangement of helpful guide, assurance of weak populaces, and cooperative endeavors to address emergencies mirror the flexibility of the human soul. This trust is grounded in the conviction that even in the midst of misfortune, the obligation to maintaining basic freedoms stays steady.

9. Gaining from Previous slip-ups:

Trust for a superior future is moored in the limit of social orders and foundations to gain from previous oversights. By recognizing authentic treacheries, legislatures and social orders can make ready for compromise, restitutions, and the foundation of frameworks that forestall the reiteration of common liberties infringement. The confident vision is one where the examples of the past add to an additional illuminated and sympathetic future.

10. A Common Obligation to Consistent Improvement:

Eventually, the most getting through wellspring of trust lies in the common responsibility of mankind to consistent improvement. States, establishments, and people are called upon to stay cautious, reflective, and versatile despite developing difficulties. The expectation is for an existence where the quest for basic liberties is certainly not a static objective however a continuous excursion, where every age expands upon the advancement of the past one, guaranteeing a tradition of equity, value, and pride for all.